MIB
MEN IN BLACK™

THE SCRIPT AND THE STORY
BEHIND THE FILM

WARNING!
UNAUTHORIZED USERS
WILL BE NEURALYZED!

MIB MEN IN BLACK™

THE SCRIPT AND THE STORY BEHIND THE FILM

Screen Story and Screenplay by Ed Solomon

Forewords by Barry Sonnenfeld and Walter F. Parkes and Laurie MacDonald

Additional Text by Diana Landau and Dawn Margolis

Photographs by Melinda Sue Gordon, Andy Schwartz, Michael O'Neill, and Industrial Light & Magic

Penguin Books

PENGUIN BOOKS

Published by the Penguin Group
Penguin Books Ltd, 27 Wrights Lane, London W8 5TZ, England
Penguin Books USA Inc., 375 Hudson Street, New York, New York 10014, USA
Penguin Books Australia Ltd, Ringwood, Victoria, Australia
Penguin Books Canada Ltd, 10 Alcorn Avenue, Toronto, Ontario, Canada M4V 3B2
Penguin Books (NZ) Ltd, 182–190 Wairau Road, Auckland 10, New Zealand

Penguin Books Ltd, Registered Offices: Harmondsworth, Middlesex, England

First published in the USA and Canada by Newmarket Press 1997
Published in Penguin 1997

3 5 7 9 10 8 6 4 2

Printed in Great Britain by Butler & Tanner Ltd, Frome, Somerset

CONTENTS

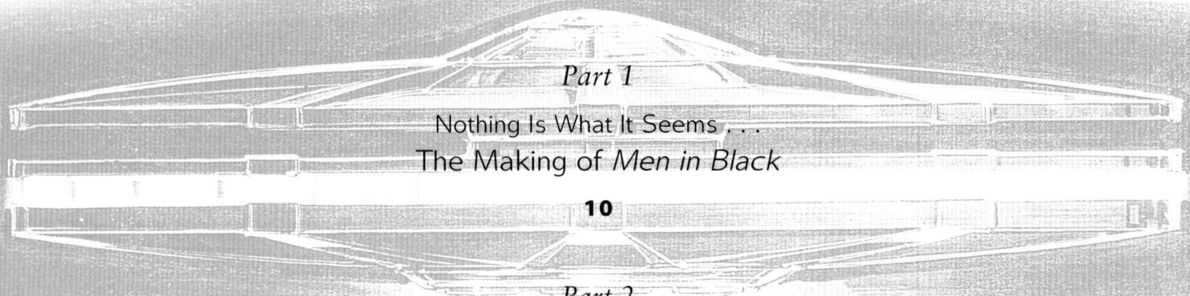

THE ALIENS ARE US

by Barry Sonnenfeld

Many people assume that I'm an alien. For one thing, I have a very warped sense of humor. For another, I've heard a rumor that people who make films about aliens actually know some things other people don't know. So I've already talked to a contractor about putting in a fence around my property, because I have a feeling I'll be getting visits from people who want me to tell them where they can meet Mikey, or Mr. Gentle, or the worm guys—because of course I know where they're living, don't I?

I can't really confirm or deny any of this. How do I know that when I'm dreaming, I'm not awake, and that when I'm awake, I'm not really dreaming?

Truthfully, as far as I know, I'm not working with any real aliens. I don't know if there *are* any aliens living here on Earth. (Now, Steven Spielberg may know something else.) And I haven't been visited or threatened by the real Men in Black, because I haven't claimed to have seen any aliens.

But I've always believed deeply in my heart that we humans don't have a clue about what's going on. I once took a college course where I learned that every single thing "experts" on the planet have ever claimed is the truth has turned out not to be true. Whether it's the notion that

Left: **At the helm of *Men in Black* is director Barry Sonnenfeld, who first made his reputation in the film industry as a cinematographer. His distinctive visual style is evident in all the films he has since directed, including the 1995 box-office hit *Get Shorty.*** ***Above:*** **The "worm aliens" created for the film are real New York characters.**

A malevolent alien from deep space streaks through the night sky above rural New York in this production sketch from the film.

the sun revolves around the earth, or that the earth is flat, or that you have to eat from the four food groups. So for us to talk as if we have firm knowledge of anything is ridiculous.

I loved the script because it was based on the idea that aliens live among us, but only a few dedicated agents know about it. I wanted to make a movie that in a light and fun way shows us that perhaps we are clueless.

To me, New York was the perfect place to make it—I've always felt that if there were aliens, New York is where they'd feel most comfortable. I see people there all the time who I'm convinced must be aliens. Shooting in New York gave us the chance to work in a lot of local color and play with some funny ideas about aliens—for example, they go to a Russian diner for a big meeting, because it turns out that all aliens love *pirogi*.

Even though the story is a fantasy, working on this movie has made me stop and wonder if it's closer to reality than we think. Since I've been involved with *Men in Black*, my wife and I have had a daughter, which has been a very life-affirming and mind-expanding experience. It's made me look outside myself, and what I thought I knew. Who knows what's really out there?

FILMING AN URBAN LEGEND

by Walter F. Parkes and Laurie MacDonald

Men in Black—how can you resist it? It's such an intriguing title. As producers, we were attracted to this project for lots of reasons. One was that it grew out of a real urban legend; it wasn't just something the comic book writers made up. We were fascinated by the theory that there exists this tiny, elite cadre of agents who hold the fate of the planet in their hands. They're the only ones who know that aliens are living among us, and the perils this poses. These guys quietly go about saving the world, but never get credit for it.

We love the the contrasts built into the story and tried to play them up. The contrast between the far-out technology the Men in Black use, and their very low-tech personal style—the boxy black suits, the old Ford LTD, and so on. The contrast between a completely real-world setting and the fantastic beings that suddenly appear in it. It's still our world . . . but one in which almost anything can happen.

Our image of the Men in Black was that they were a lot like the New York street cops in *The French Connection,* or other movies in that style. They're tired and world-weary. The coffee has gone cold. But instead of staking out a drug deal, they're staking out some deposed sur-prefect from Alpha Centauri. The key is: they treat him the same as they would treat any petty criminal. That's part of their coolness.

The Men in Black legend exists in several different versions, and we were able to incorporate different aspects of it. For example, some say that they are agents of the federal government but unknown to virtually everyone else in government. That's the conspiracy theory. Others claim that the MIB are really aliens themselves—and that's why they look so strange and stiff and unhip. We didn't portray them like that, but we married the two ideas by having some aliens employed at the MIB headquarters.

We took the opportunity in developing the script to make the characters more complex and interesting. The comic book was more straightforward, hard action. But we wanted to go deeper, to show the real burden on the Men in Black of their knowledge. The idea that once you know some terrible secret, you can't "unknow" it. Very early on, we decided to show one character who chooses to go back to real life, to be purged of his knowledge, while the other one is learning how the world works. You look for things like that—simple character dynamics that you can hang all the bells and whistles on. We really wanted this movie to be more about the Men in Black than the aliens.

But there's also an irresistible appeal in the concept that almost anyone might be an alien.

Will Smith portrays Agent Jay, a new recruit to the Men in Black.

It could be some well-known public figure…or someone you know. The scenario we always imagine is: you're driving along late at night, in some city, and you look in the window of an all-night laundromat, and you see some guy in there, just watching his clothes go round and round in the dryer. And you can't help but think: what planet is he from?

This story provides the answer. When you walk out of the movie theatre, you might very well look at the world in a different way.

Above: **Men in Black agents Kay, Zed, and Jay.** ***Below:*** **The alien immigration center at MIB headquarters.**

Nothing
is what
it
seems...
THE MAKING OF
MEN IN BLACK

WHO ARE THE MEN IN BLACK?

Above: **Tommy Lee Jones and Will Smith star as a pair of elite cops monitoring alien activity on Earth.** ***Below:*** **"Lacertiliac humanoids" Mavis 12 and her offspring Mavis 13, two of the wide variety of alien life forms created for** ***Men in Black.***

WHO ARE THE MEN IN BLACK, and how did they find their way onto the movie screen?

The Men in Black are a team of "over-the-hill guys in retro suits who know how the universe works," says Producer Walter F. Parkes of Amblin Entertainment. "They are apocryphal agents, cosmic G-men and gunslingers, and very cool, savvy guys."

They strive to seem ordinary, to blend in, to move through the world unnoticed—but in fact, they have one of the most important jobs in the world, not to mention one of the weirdest. They monitor and police extraterrestrial aliens who land on Earth—some to seek asylum, others for more nefarious purposes. Part of the Men in Black's mission, therefore, is "protecting the Earth from the scum of the universe."

Another part is to cover up all evidence of this alien presence. Any human who stumbles on such evidence receives a visit from the Men in Black (usually known as MIB), and is persuaded that it's a figment of their imagination, or perhaps a stray byproduct of swamp gas. And if they can't be persuaded, their memory of the event is simply erased.

The MIB operate out of a high-tech headquarters in lower Manhattan, camouflaged behind an anonymous exterior. They use ultra-sophisticated technology to track aliens and agents; wield weapons beyond the wildest dreams of any army on the planet; and drive large, nondescript black sedans that transform into gravity-defying magic carpets at the push of a button. They have no real names, no fami-

***Above:* A spaceship piloted by the villainous Edgar Bug smashes through the Unisphere, a landmark of the 1964 World's Fair in New York, scene of the film's climax. *Right:* "Agent Kay" holds a neuralyzer, the MIB's trademark "memory eraser."**

lies, no official identities—no life outside the MIB.

Where did such characters, such a setting, and such an extraordinary story line come from? Even though this is their first appearance on a movie screen, the Men in Black have been around for some time. The incarnation of MIB on view in this Columbia Pictures/ Amblin Entertainment release is the result of a collaboration among some of the film industry's brightest talents: in writing, producing, directing, designing, and acting. But even further back, it was born in the imagination of a young writer steeped in sci-fi movies and the TV spy and cop shows of the 1960s, and fascinated by the rumor—barely an underground whisper—of a secret organization called the Men in Black.

GENESIS

"'It's always the juxtapostion of the tawdry and miraculous. The MIB are as low-tech as you can get in their personal style, completely detached from everything in our culture that's thought to be 'cutting-edge.' Yet walking around with the burden of knowing how the universe works. How it can all end in one second. Those elements are at the heart of it."

—*Producer Walter F. Parkes*

IN THE SUMMER OF 1992, producers Walter F. Parkes and Laurie MacDonald—currently co-heads of movie production for DreamWorks SKG—optioned a little-known comic book series called *The Men in Black*, created and written by Lowell Cunningham. Only three issues of the comic existed, but it was enough to attract Parkes and MacDonald to its premise: of human protagonists doing battle with the extraordinary in our everyday world.

"So many comic book properties deal with superheroes or strange creatures as their main characters, which can be limiting," notes Parkes "But what attracted us to *Men in Black* was that it centered on very human characters, operating in the real world but with some fantasy elements. We had these extraordinarily cool agents who use human strength and intelligence to battle alien creatures."

That essential quality of the story was what made it seem right for Steven Spielberg's Amblin Entertainment. "We had been asked by Steven to come and run his production company, and we felt that *Men in Black* was a good fit," Parkes comments. "Amblin has always been associated with high-end family entertainment that integrates really good stories with state-of-the-art technology. It's important that the human element doesn't get lost among the creatures and the high-tech environment." Spielberg himself would serve as executive producer, keeping a benevolent eye on the production but giving a free hand to his creative team led by Parkes and MacDonald.

The comic book suggested to the filmmakers the overall tone they would aim for—cool, world-weary, and more than a little retro—as well as the general outlines of the main characters. "The imagery

Left: **Walter F. Parkes and Laurie MacDonald are the producers responsible for bringing *Men in Black* to the screen, shortly after they assumed leadership of movie production for DreamWorks SKG. *Opposite:* Part of the set design for the MIB Headquarters, conceived to look simultaneously retro and futuristic.**

suggested that juxtaposition of a kind of retro organization set against a futuristic group of aliens," says MacDonald. Some specifics found their way into the script as well; for example, the idea that the MIB acquire their far-out technology from the aliens they police, and finance their operation by holding patents on inventions "imported" from outer space—like CDs and velcro.

Still, notes Laurie MacDonald, "the comic book was a starting place. Not many people had seen

Above: **Director Barry Sonnenfeld, left, with executive producer Steven Spielberg on the set of *Men in Black*. *Below:* Cover art by Sandy Carruthers from one of the original *The Men in Black* comic books. Used by arrangement with Marvel Entertainment**

it," so the filmmakers were at liberty to adapt freely—which can be more problematic if there's already a huge audience intimately familiar with details of a comic book. Also, says MacDonald, "it was quite different from making a movie that rides on the success of a famous, established comic like *Batman*. Here, we just saw a great movie premise that we could develop."

THE MAKING OF AN URBAN LEGEND

"I hear the music, daylight disc,
Three men in black said 'Don't report this.'"
Blue Oyster Cult

LOWELL CUNNINGHAM, the creator of *The Men in Black* comic, vividly recalls his first encounter with the Men in Black myth, a recurring theme in the annals of the paranormal since the 1950s.

"I was driving around my home town of Knoxville with my friend Dennis Matheson, who has a strong interest in UFO phenomena. We saw a huge black sedan cruise past us—a Cadillac or Lincoln, maybe—and it really stood out, because we were in the student neighborhood near the University of Tennessee, where there usually aren't many big cars. Dennis casually commented, 'Oh, that's just like the cars the Men in Black drive,' and I had to get him to explain who the Men in Black were. I was so fascinated by the idea I just went on a tear, developing my own background to fit the UFO legends. The comic grew from there."

The original myth of the "men in black" has changed very little since it first surfaced. Its existence has been documented in parascientific journals, books, and more recently on the Internet. It seems that in 1953, the founder of an organization called the International Flying Saucer Bureau (IFSB) announced in the group's journal *Space Review* that he had discovered the solution to the "mystery of flying saucers." He'd like nothing better than to publish this information, Albert K. Bender wrote, but he has been strongly warned not to do so—by a "higher source."

Bender would say only that he had been visited by three "members of the U.S. government ...wearing dark suits," who had fully briefed

Above:* Shooting on location in Manhattan; Linda Fiorentino and Will Smith with the MIB's Ford LTD "supercar." *Below:* Poster for a 1950s science-fiction movie *Earth vs. the Flying Saucers*, a Columbia Pictures release starring Hugh Marlowe and Joan Taylor. *Courtesy Ron Borst/ Hollywood Movie Posters

An Interview with Lowell Cunningham,
Creator of the *Men in Black* Comic Book

Q: What led you to create the series "The Men in Black"?

LC: A friend of mine is interested in UFO phenomena and he told me of various rumors and legends surrounding UFOs. The most fascinating stories involved mysterious men dressed in black who invariably appeared after any UFO contact. I thought this would be a great idea for a series.

Q: I see. But your series doesn't focus on UFOs.

LC: Right. I changed that for two reasons. First, I decided that the main reason the Men in Black existed was to suppress socially explosive incidents, and that should include more than just UFOs. Anything that could upset the normal flow of society should attract their attention. The second reason is that I thought UFOs every issue might get boring after a while.

Q: So you used the legends as a jumping-off point?

LC: Yes. There's quite a bit of lore on the MIB organization, but nothing on individual agents. Pretty much all I've kept from the popular mythology are the clothes, the cars, and some of their methods. Their mission is quite a bit different.

Q: What about your heroes, Jay and Kay?

LC: I'm not sure I'd call Kay a hero; his motivations aren't especially admirable. For that matter, Jay is constantly in danger of becoming like Kay. That's part of the continuing story.

Q: So you think a hero is someone who does the right things for the right reasons?

LC: Pretty much. Jay tries to do the right things for the right reasons, but sometimes does the wrong thing—still for the right reasons. Just about everything Kay does is for the wrong reasons. Kay likes the power of his position and, as the saying goes, power corrupts.

Q: Do you think something like the Men in Black actually exists?

LC: If it does, I hope someone like Jay is in charge ...Who can say? If it does exist, we'd only know about it if it didn't do a good job covering its tracks. I'm mainly interested in playing "what if." If the MIB actually did exist, what would they do, how would they do it, and so on.

Q: You seem to have given Jay and Kay carte blanche.

LC: You mean in equipment and other resources? I guess so, but an organization operating over and above the rest of the world would need agents who could go anywhere and do anything.

Q: Then can we expect to see Jay and Kay in bizarre locations?

LC: I don't know. I think it's interesting to see weird things happening in average, boring locations. It brings things closer to home if you think monsters are just down the street than if you see them thousands of miles away. You'd be surprised what really goes on in small towns and neighborhoods. America is an interesting country.

Q: Like in that ancient Chinese curse "May you live interesting times."

LC: Exactly. We live in interesting times—but it could be worse. Maybe we need an organization like the MIB.

Q: Because so many weird things are going on?

LC: Sure. I mean, look at some of the things reported in the media. There's the Gator Man over in South Carolina. In Europe there's a "ghost crossing" on one highway. In big cities, convenience stores are being held up by nude men who steal clothes....Here in Tennessee there's a musician who claims to be artistically inspired by aliens. And that's just what makes it into the news. Who knows what else is going on?

Q: You must really keep up with the news.

LC: I think truth really can be stranger than fiction. A lot of what I've written for this series was inspired by news stories. The drug cults is Issue 1, and the supernatural elements of Issue 3 were loosely based on actual news items. Whenever I hear about something which is dismissed as hysteria or sensation, I immediately think, "But what if it really did happen?"

—Reprinted from The Men in Black *#1, January 1990*

Above: **Concept art created by the production design team shows key set elements and scenes, here, the top of one of the World's Fair towers—a spacecraft in the film—lifting off.** ***Right:*** **The stars of "The Man from U.N.C.L.E.," a hit 1960s TV spy show that inspired Lowell Cunningham.**
Courtesy Ron Borst/Hollywood Movie Posters

him on the matter of flying saucers and then threatened him with prison if he ever repeated a word of what he'd been told. Bender finally detailed his experiences in a 1962 book, *Flying Saucers and the Three Men*, in which he described, among other things, being taken to the South Pole in an alien spacecraft, and the "three men" suddenly materializing in his bedroom.

None of this enhanced Bender's credibility much, but it did gradually give rise to an intriguing notion—that the men in black were not government agents at all, but aliens themselves! (Parkes and MacDonald incorporated this idea

An Encounter with the MIB?

At 8:15 a.m., February 22, 1967, Connie Carpenter left the house to go to school. As she started to walk down the street a large black car pulled up alongside her. She later identified it as a 1949 Buick. The occupant of the car opened the door and beckoned to her. Thinking that he was seeking directions, she approached him. He was a young, clean-cut man of about twenty-five, wearing a colorful Mod shirt, no jacket (it was bitter cold), had neatly combed hair and appeared to be suntanned. There was a very interesting detail: she said the car appeared to be brand new inside and out even though it was a vintage model. This detail has cropped up many times in our "Men in Black" cases. Some of these cars even smell new inside, according to various witnesses.

When she reached the automobile, the driver suddenly lunged and grabbed her arm, ordering her to get in with him. She fought back and there was a brief struggle before she finally broke away. She ran back to the house and locked herself in, completely terrified.

Connie remained indoors the following day, February 23. At 3:00 p.m. she heard someone on the porch, and there was a loud knock on the door. She went to it cautiously and found a note had been slipped under it. It was written in pencil in block letters on a piece of ordinary notebook paper. "Be careful girl," it read, "I can get you yet."

—*from* The Complete Guide to Mysterious Beings *by John A. Keel*

into their movie: the agents don't really turn out to be aliens, but aliens do work in the MIB headquarters, and move around on Earth disguised as humans.)

Although Bender's is the first specific reference to the MIB, the image of menacing, dark-garbed figures has much deeper roots, harking back to ancient times and to many cultures. There are Middle Eastern traditions of men in black robes and turbans trying to lure people into the desert with sinister intent; tales in Europe of black-clad beings wandering the countryside engaging in vampirism; and a long-standing myth in China of a superior race of beings who live under the earth's surface and send out emissaries dressed in black to observe and manipulate human affairs. Some Native Americans feared a malicious "black man" who lurked in the forest, and scholars even find MIB overtones in Nathaniel Hawthorne's short story "Young Goodman Brown."

At all events, since the eccentric Bender first encountered them, mysterious men in black have cropped up on many occasions in which people claim to have evidence of extraterrestrial life. These "silencers," as Bender later called them, generally travel in teams of two or three, and their main purpose seems to be to discourage—or actively deter—UFO and alien spotters from reporting what they have experienced.

A typical MIB encounter goes something like this: Soon after witnessing

***Preceding pages:* An MIB clean-up team prepares to create a diversion after a rogue alien has been "terminated" in a shower of blue goo. *Left:* Tommy Lee Jones hefts a Series 4 De-Atomizer, an MIB-style shotgun.**

some sort of paranormal phenomenon, the witness is visited by one or more strange men. They wear black suits (in outdated styles, sometimes made of an unrecognizable fabric), black ties, and white shirts; and they drive older yet immaculate luxury cars. Often they claim to be from one government agency or another, and flash cryptic identification cards or badges. (Always upon further investigation, the agency claims to have no record of said agents, or itself turns out not to exist.)

The "agents" tend to display not only uncanny knowledge about what the witness has seen, but intimate personal knowledge of the witness. Sometimes their faces are obscured by a hat brim and dark glasses; what's visible tends to be ghostly pale (some reports mention "Asiatic" features, very thin or nonexistent lips, hairlessness, or even more bizarre physical traits.) They may walk only in straight lines, speak in a mechanical monotone, and their "interviews" often turn into Mickey Spillane-style interrogations complete with gangster-tinged speech and threats. Small wonder that people have been reduced by panic by these encounters, or that some insist the Men in Black are not of this world!

The U.S. government, by the way, has come close to officially recognizing the existence of the MIB. In 1967, the then Assistant Chief of Staff of the U.S. Air Force sent a memo to various defense agencies, reading as follows: "Information, not verifiable, has reached Hq USAF that persons claiming to represent the Air Force or other Defense establishments have contacted citizens who have sighted unidentified flying objects. In one reported case an individual in civilian clothes, who represented himself as a member of NORAD, demanded and received photos belonging to a private citizen.…All military personnel…who hear of such reports should immediately notify their local OSI office."

For "his" Men in Black, Lowell Cunningham used what appealed to him from the welter of legend and "information" out there. He liked the ideas about their clothes, their cars, and their generally retro style. He chose as their main mission the suppression of dangerous information—not only about UFOs but any socially disturbing phenomena. And he began to develop individual personae for his characters: Kay, the older, harder, seen-it-all agent; and the up-and-coming Jay, who has all the right stuff for MIB work but still clings to his ideals. Those personalities have made their way onto the screen in remarkably similar form. But the process was a long and complex one, involving major decisions about scripting, scene-setting, casting, and interpretation. And as usual, it all begins with the screenplay.

A full-size model of the alien spaceship gapes open after crashing at the World's Fair site.

FROM COMIC TO SCREEN

LIKE ANY TRULY CREATIVE FILM, *Men in Black* took its eventual shape from the tastes, instincts, and experience of its principal creators. Early on, producers Parkes and MacDonald brought in screenwriter Ed Solomon to help shape the basic material and premise of the comic book into a shooting script for a major movie. Solomon, whose film credits include the screenplays for *Bill and Ted's Excellent Adventure* and *Leaving Normal*, was also one of the original writers for TV's *It's Garry Shandling's Show*.

It's no accident that the producers tapped a comedy writer for the task. "The original tone of the comic was tougher and more violent. It was right for that medium, but we always had in mind to bring out the comedy more," recalls Laurie MacDonald.

Ed Solomon's first contact with *Men in Black* was a phone call from Walter Parkes, telling him about an intriguing little property he thought might take six weeks to flesh into a script. Solomon didn't know Parkes but had heard good things about him. He would come to know him very well indeed over the course of what stretched into nearly four *years* of work on the film.

Solomon was at first dubious about a "comic book movie," but only a little way into his reading of the Lowell Cunningham 'zines began to get excited and make notes about ideas and directions. "It intrigued me right away, got me thinking about issues like how we humans fit into the bigger scheme of things. Then I started thinking of ways to put it into a comedic perspective." He outlined an opening scene or two, met with Parkes, who pronounced it a good

Below: **Concept art of the MIB supercar in its fully transformed state.** ***Opposite:*** **Agents Jay and Kay confront the Edgar Bug at the film's climax.**

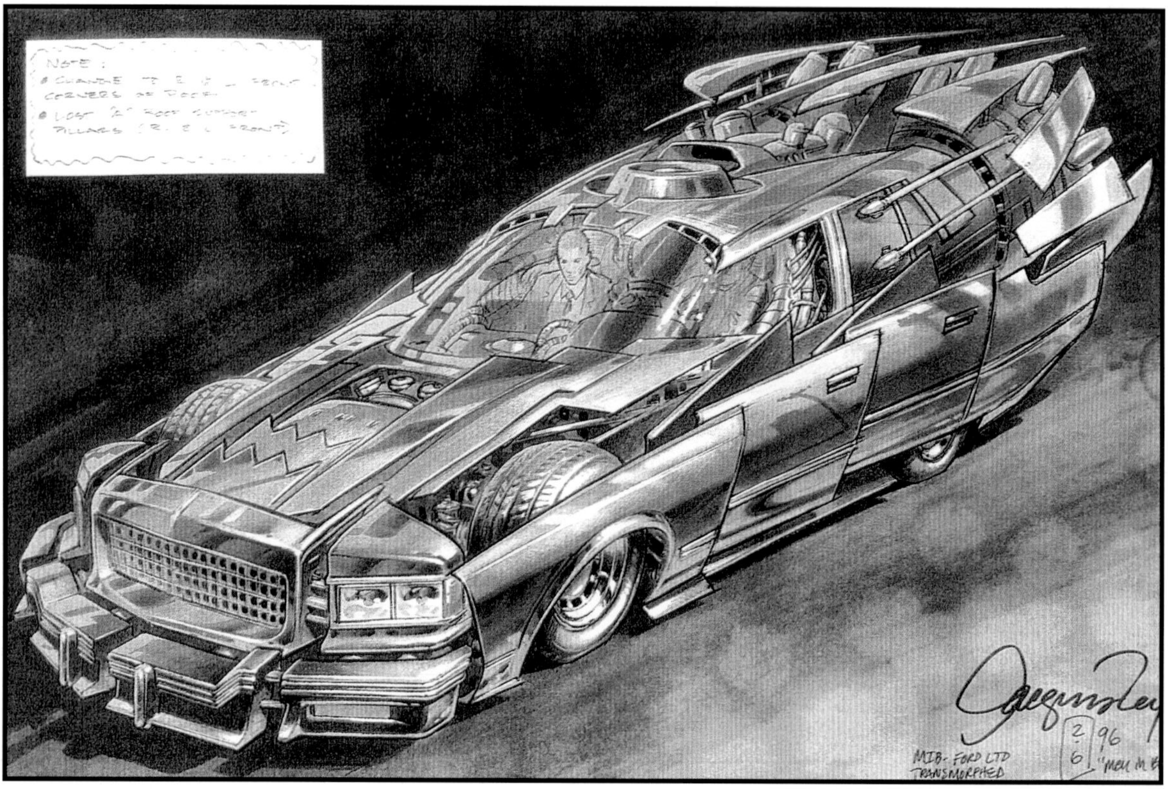

Storyboarding the Script

Storyboards are a vital step in any film's journey from script to screen. Director Barry Sonnenfeld worked with a storyboard artist to map out camera angles, moves, cuts, and countless other details of how each shot and sequence will unfold. Here, near the film's end, the evil space bug bursts free of his human disguise as the Men in Black agents watch.

start, and they were off. It was a fruitful partnership, with Parkes's instinct for mainstream entertainment and Solomon's more loopy sensibility complementing each other.

A problem they encountered, says Solomon, "was that the basic idea could go off in so many different directions. We started with what we thought was a clear approach—we were sure it was a comedy—but soon so many variants emerged, it was hard to know which to stick with. That great flexibility in both story line and tone was both a blessing and a curse."

One goal they always agreed on was that the film should have both mainstream appeal and an edge of strangeness, it should seem both familiar and utterly unique. "The story had to be less strange than the characters," says Solomon. "We tried to create a story line with a relatively familiar structure, so we could overlay it with these incredibly strange characters without the audience getting lost. We wanted to exploit all the 'two cops on a beat' genre conventions, and appeal to sci-fi lovers at the same time."

Around the time a first draft script was completed, Barry Sonnenfeld signed on to direct *Men in Black,* and star Tommy Lee Jones became involved. Sonnenfeld contributed his ideas at that stage but soon had to depart for another project. Jones liked the material, but favored a slight shift in tone to make the story a little darker, more along the lines of Robert Heinlein's science fiction. If he liked the rewrite, Jones would commit to the project—a giant step forward. He did...and he did.

But the real turning point, Solomon feels, was when director Barry Sonnenfeld rejoined the production team after a year's hiatus. Sonnenfeld became Solomon's chief collaborator on the later drafts—there would be nearly a dozen by the end—and subtly urged the writing back toward a more comic vein. While there were inevitable spells of burnout and discouragement in these latter stages, it became clear to the writer that this large, potentially unwieldy film was now in the most capable of hands.

"You often hear stories about these big summer pictures going out of control, people fighting, the film turning into garbage. To me, it all depends on the strength of the person holding the reins. Barry was brilliantly able to take all the disparate voices and talents involved in *Men in Black* and focus them, use them to sharpen his own vision rather than diffuse it." In that evaluation, all the key players in the project concur.

Solomon stayed on board during the entire four-year span it took to bring *Men in Black* to the screen, and credits the producers and Sonnenfeld for making it a great experience. "It's the first time I've worked on a film where the final result was far more creative, more festive and fun, more visually interesting and intricate than I could have imagined."

Concept art of the rogue alien Mikey, classified by the MIB as an "amphibious bipedal bovine."

NO CASH
KEYS
I ♥ NY
49¢
PLANET
FACIAL TISSUE
TWO PLY
FINEST QUALITY
AUTO-HOUSE

THE DIRECTOR'S DEADPAN TOUCH

ONCE THEY HAD A DRAFT SCREENPLAY, producers Parkes and MacDonald set to work assembling a production team. The first and most critical decision was, who would direct? They needed someone who would feel an affinity with the material that matched their own, yet who would bring a strong personal vision and a distinctive tone to the finished film.

Again they took their cue from character: the Men in Black and their mission. Says Walter Parkes: "Even though the comic book itself wasn't funny, there's something inherently funny about the situation of these classic tough-guy cops getting heavy with the guys they're policing—because the guys are aliens. The MIB just go about their business, paying no attention to that bizarre fact. It calls for a kind of deadpan attitude. That's what led us to Barry Sonnenfeld, because he's really the leading practitioner of that style. Barry is a comic director who doesn't rely on jokes. He relies on understanding the comic situation and playing it absolutely straight."

Laurie MacDonald elaborates on the choice: "There are very few directors we felt were right for this movie. Barry was at the top of a very short list because so few can combine the sense of style it needed, the comic tone, the sophisticated underplay behind the action." Screenwriter Ed Solomon echoes this opinion: "Really it was Barry's blend of visual acuity and sense of humor that put the ultimate stamp on this movie."

Sonnenfeld, whose directorial credits include the 1995 hit comedy *Get Shorty*, and the two *Addams Family* movies, read the draft script as early as 1993 and expressed strong interest in taking on *Men in Black*. "My wife read it too," says Sonnenfeld. "We read scripts together, and we both immediately loved the idea of the movie." But right around that time, *Get Shorty* was green-lighted, and Sonnenfeld became unavailable for a large chunk of time. By 1995, when *Men in Black* was finally ready to go into production, he was again free and ready to hit the ground running.

Above: **The director and his stars confer on the set.** ***Below:*** **One of the "worm aliens" that inhabit the MIB Headquarters. These "slackers" of the extraterrestrial world crave caffeine and hang out in the coffee room.** ***Opposite:*** **Guess which one is the alien? A New York street scene from the film.**

"There's something inherently funny about the situation of these classic tough-guy cops getting heavy with the guys they're policing—because the guys are aliens. It calls for a kind of deadpan attitude. That's what led us to Barry Sonnenfeld, because he's really the leading practitioner of that style. Barry is a comic director who doesn't rely on jokes. He relies on understanding the comic situation and playing it absolutely straight."

—*Walter F. Parkes*

Director Barry Sonnenfeld works with actor John Alexander, who plays the alien Mikey. A veteran body-suit performer, Alexander has endured the discomfort of being packed into strange disguises designed by Rick Baker for fifteen years. This one contains leg extensions to make Mikey tall; inside, it's hard both to see and breathe.

"As director, Barry Sonnenfeld pushes the project toward a higher level of sophistication," comments Parkes. "Visually he's very sophisticated, yet he also has a pretty pitch about where the laugh is. The tone of this movie was not an easy target."

Nor were the logistical challenges it posed. Its emphasis on character aside, *Men in Black* is a big, complicated effects film, with aspects of production that call for great technical expertise and directorial coordination to bring off successfully. It has big action "set pieces" with

lots of production and set design; an enormous amount of special effects, including CGI (computer-generated imaging) and puppet work.

"It's easy for the movie to be overshadowed by all those details," remarks Walter Parkes. "The movie becomes *about* the effects, and we didn't want that. Barry was able to balance all the movie's values successfully. The design, effects, and so on were all in service of the story and the characters, not vice versa. It's a very difficult thing for a director to pull off." Adds Laurie MacDonald, "He's delivering all we had envisioned. So often as producer you feel, as the film's being made, that it's not quite what you had in mind. But this has the feel of the movie we'd hoped for."

Sonnenfeld credits his production team for much of the endeavor's success. The impressive crew includes cinematographer Don Peterman, with whom Sonnenfeld worked on *Addams Family Values* and *Get Shorty;* production designer Bo Welch; set decorator Cheryl Carasik; costume designer Mary Vogt; and editor Jim Miller (*Men in Black* was his fifth collaboration with the director). And of course, the wizards at Industrial Light & Magic, who handled the vast array of visual effects the film demanded. "All these people are fantastic, the best of anyone you could want in those positions," raves Sonnenfeld. "The reason it's been so easy is because all these people are so prepared and professional. So we've been incredibly lucky."

Not to mention having Steven Spielberg as executive producer, he adds. "Working with Steven was both thrilling and scary because I was constantly wondering what he would say—for example, about my choice of how an alien should look. But very early on he said, don't worry about what Steven would say. And he seems to like everything."

Sonnenfeld's collaborators return the compliments. Comments production designer Bo Welch: "He's the most prepared director I've ever worked with. He has endless energy and a really unusual sense of humor. Barry publishes shot lists—something few directors do, but which is really helpful in planning ahead and tracking what you've done. And he's very knowledgeable and facile with effects photography."

The director, as it should be, has the last word: "Just get a good script, surround yourself with great actors, and there's very little a director can do to mess up a movie—except not understand the tone." No one doubts that Sonnenfeld understood that from the beginning.

Above: **Concept art of the tiny "universe" fought over by warring worlds.** ***Below:*** **Director of photography Don Peterman, a two-time Academy Award nominee for his work on** ***Flashdance*** **and** ***Star Trek IV: The Voyage Home.***

THE LOOK OF THE FILM

PRINCIPAL PHOTOGRAPHY for *Men in Black* began in mid-March 1996. The film followed a seventeen-week production schedule, filming on local locations around Los Angeles and on five Sony Pictures soundstages, before moving to New York for several weeks of filming on practical locations in and around Manhattan.

Except for an opening scene that takes place somewhere on the Mexican border, and two brief forays into rural upstate New York, the whole of *Men in Black* is set in New York City. This makes perfect sense, of course. As Walter Parkes points out, New York is the ultimate meeting place of the weird and the very cool, a culture that takes the unexpected in stride—even including an invasion from outer space.

Barry Sonnenfeld, a native New Yorker, felt instinctively from the start that *Men in Black* should take place in his home city. The original draft of the script, he notes, called for many different locations, from Kansas to Nevada to Washington, D.C. to Los Angeles. "But my feeling was always to centralize it in New York." In part this was because "if there are aliens on this planet, New York is where they'd feel comfortable and blend in."

Another factor was the filmmakers' desire to link *Men in Black* with the darkly comic "police procedural" films of the 1970s, in which the New York milieu inescapably set the mood. They name *The French Connection,* with Gene Hackman as Popeye Doyle, as the archetype of such films, which also include *Serpico* and *Prince of the City.* "Only here," says Sonnenfeld, "when you're shaking down a guy in a bar, you're shaking down an alien. But you never acknowledge that it's anything

Right: **Agents Jay (Will Smith), Zed (Rip Torn), and Kay (Tommy Lee Jones) check the giant screen on which the MIB track the whereabouts of all aliens on Earth.**

Production designer Bo Welch received Academy Award nominations for his work on *A Little Princess* and *The Color Purple*.

strange; you just talk to him like any street criminal. And therein lies the comedy, we hope."

New York also offers, as Sonnenfeld and others point out, the bonus of being able to walk around and see events, people, even buildings that make you stop and wonder. "Things you can't make sense of," the director says.

"Like on Fifth Avenue in the fifties, there are these strange silver tanks, about seven feet high and two feet thick, with a hose going into the ground. What are they for? Someone told me they're 'cooling the AT&T cables.' Well, that makes as much sense to me as if someone had said 'they're alien decompression tanks.' And down near Battery Park, there's this strange, gigantic building that I'm told is the 'vent room' for the Holland Tunnel. They have to pump fresh air down there so drivers don't asphyxiate. But our conceit in the movie is that this building is the MIB headquarters."

The distinctly sixties retro environment of the MIB was created by production designer Bo Welch, a two-time Academy Award nominee who has received critical acclaim for his ability to blend fantasy and reality. Welch recalls that "when I first read script I thought it was very cool, but I wasn't available. I put it aside but it haunted me—it seemed like a great opportunity and I really liked Barry's work. So when the chance came around again, I jumped on it."

Sonnenfeld, for his part, remembers being dubious that Welch would want the assignment. "I told him it was reality-based and would look very ordinary; there wouldn't be much for him to do. But he said, 'Barry, it's the best script out there and I'm going to do this movie.' Welch was further tempted when the director mentioned his preference for using wide lenses to capture all the details of a scene. "That was music to my ears, because it means there's less chance a lot of effort will be wasted. Sometimes designers get grief for building a set that's never seen on film."

The production designer, as Welch describes the job, is in charge of all the things put in front of the camera "other than the actors' faces and what they do with their bodies. All the visual aspects of the film: props and vehicles, set and

"It's hard designing guns, and we had a lot of them to do. There have been so many done, and they have to seem functional. But it's an interesting challenge."

—*Bo Welch*

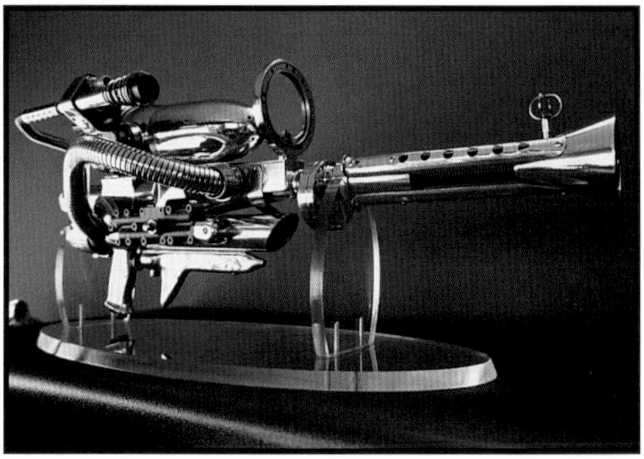

locations, are your responsibility. You have to interact closely with wardrobe and transportation and lighting. Basically, you're responsible for the look of the movie. And sometimes you get into designing shots."

Welch also loves shooting in New York, and hates "trying to fake New York on a set." Like Sonnenfeld, he appreciates the "great visual stimuli you get just from walking around, ideas you file away and use later." Welch was especially happy to be able to use the Guggenheim Museum as a backdrop for one of the scenes, because he always thought it looked like a stack of flying saucers.

One of the principal sets for the film is the MIB Headquarters, an homage to 1960s corporate architecture and a vision of the future as it might have been imagined in 1964. The exterior for MIB HQ was the Lower Manhattan utility building described by Sonnenfeld, while the interior set was constructed on Sony soundstages 12 and 15—the largest continuous soundstage in the world, where movies like *The Wizard of Oz* and *Hook* were filmed.

Like the other film masters involved with *Men in Black*, Welch set his personal stamp on the film—and nowhere more so than in this set. "The final conception of the MIB HQ was something I helped decide. I saw their headquarters as a kind of alien Ellis Island or arrivals terminal, where they would come in and out, go through checkpoints, as well as where the MIB agents work." For the interior design, Welch's main inspiration was the great Finnish architect Eero Saarinen, who designed

Above: **Director Barry Sonnenfeld sizes up a location shot in Lower Manhattan; in the background are the World Trade Towers.** ***Overleaf:*** **In the interview room of the MIB Headquarters, prospective Men in Black—the elite from every branch of the military and law enforcement—are put through their paces.**

"Our basis for the retro, sixties look of the movie comes partly from the comic book but also from the absurdity, the shock of realizing that there are aliens among us. That is, once you've seen aliens, you can stop worrying about a lot of other things: like fashion—oh, please, you're telling me that wide ties are out?—or what music you should be listening to. They just become meaningless. So part of the Men in Black's cool is their utter indifference to what's current. They've got bigger things on their minds."

—Barry Sonnenfeld

the famous "winged" TWA terminal at JFK Airport, as well as the St. Louis Arch.

Welch started with that idea for the interior and then went looking for the exterior to go with it, "which is the opposite of how you usually work. In the draft script the building was described as a series of brownstones that had been gutted. On paper, that may have sounded right, but I felt that visually it wasn't clean or strong enough." (Screenwriter Ed Solomon, far from objecting to his concept being overruled, points to this as an example of how fortunate he felt to be collaborating with colleagues as talented as Welch: "I saw instantly what he meant, and it worked.")

Welch and Sonnenfeld began scouting around Manhattan for the right exterior location, and as they were driving down the West Side Highway, they turned a corner and Welch suddenly pointed to a ventilation tower. "It was essentially a big concrete block, very plain. But what's fun is that it's in the oldest part of Manhattan, surrounded by big old buildings, which makes it really stand out. And it's appropriately located at the foot of the island, right across the water from Ellis Island and the Statue of Liberty, so it's a logical place for immigrants to come into New York."

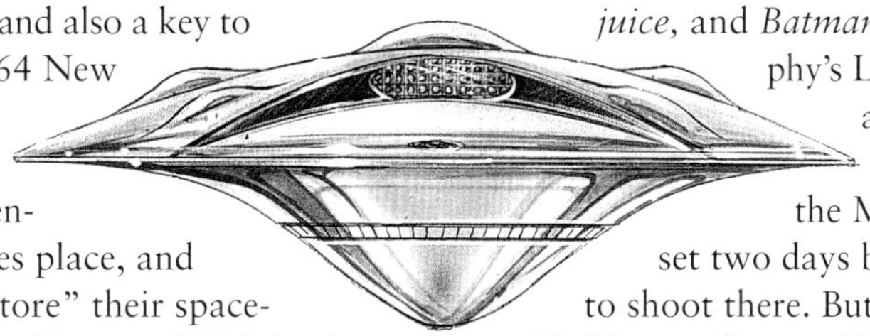

Another key set—and also a key to the plot—was the 1964 New York World's Fair. In the movie, this is where the first alien encounter on Earth takes place, and where those aliens "store" their spaceships, because they blend in so well. Distinctive structures from the Fair still stand on a site in Flushing Meadows, very near Shea Stadium, where the Mets play. (The stadium figures in another delightful plot twist.) The World's Fair link gave Welch another strong design cue.

"What struck me about that World's Fair is that it expressed such a spirit of optimism about the future—especially about space travel. This was the time when that excitement really peaked, the last time in history when most Americans seemed motivated to pursue those goals. And the Fair also expressed a kind of triumph of the human spirit that's appealing and charming...and a little funny at the same time."

Because he was occupied with another film, Welch joined the MIB team late in pre-production, making for a shorter time frame than other big movie he had designed. (These include *A Little Princess,* Mike Nichols' *The Birdcage and Wolf,* and Tim Burton's *Edward Scissorhands, Beetlejuice,* and *Batman Returns.*) True to Murphy's Law, problems cropped up at critical times, such as a sprinkler flood in the MIB headquarters set two days before they were due to shoot there. But Welch and his team, aided by art director Tom Duffield, set director Cheryl Carasik, and property master Doug Harlocker, weren't deterred.

Even the most difficult design elements—according to Welch, the long polished aluminum columns in the MIB headquarters, meant to look like streamlined rockets or javelins—were viewed as a challenge. "I often try to draw things that I think are virtually impossible to make, just to see if we can make them. That's how design can stretch itself."

***Opposite:* A concept sketch of the MIB Headquarters. *Above:* One of many spacecraft designs considered for the film. *Below:* The very '60s-looking coffee room at MIB HQ with its usual denizens, the worm aliens.**

MEET THE PLAYERS

"It's always about the cast and the words."
Barry Sonnenfeld

TAKING THE LEAD ROLES in *Men in Black* are Tommy Lee Jones as Kay, a world-weary founding member of the MIB, and Will Smith, as the hot young NYPD detective who is recruited as his partner, Jay. Also featured are Linda Fiorentino as Dr. Laurel Weaver, a New York City medical examiner unwittingly drawn into the plot while investigating a spate of unusual corpses; and Vincent D'Onofrio as Edgar, a malevolent space creature who "borrows" the body of a nasty redneck in order to carry out his evil mission on Earth. Rip Torn appears as Zed, the senior MIB agent who directs operations from headquarters.

Declares Barry Sonnenfeld: "Tommy Lee and Will are perfect for their roles." Producer Laurie MacDonald elaborates. "Tommy is a wonderful anchor for the film as an actor who isn't a comedian or known for comedy roles, but plays them masterfully," she notes. "And Will brings complete authenticity to a comic role."

Part of what first attracted the producers to the project, says Walter Parkes, is that it gave them an opportunity to create characters that could, in turn, attract really interesting actors. "Then the question became: do you cast comedians who can act, or actors who can do comedy? We opted for the latter. Since we're trying to suggest that the story is happening in the real world, we wanted to have the cast grounded in reality. And Tommy Lee Jones certainly provides that."

Jones signed on to the project very early, even before the director. His early involvement was a gift to the producers and screenwriter Ed Solomon, who not only had the benefit of this thoughtful

Tommy Lee Jones as Agent Kay shows Will Smith (at this point in the film still known as New York cop James Edwards) the high-tech gear brought to MIB by visiting aliens.

Above: Agent Kay explains the use of a neuralyzer to Edwards. Below: The first meeting between Dr. Laurel Weaver, played by Linda Fiorentino, and James Edwards (Will Smith).

actor's comments on the script, but were able to write dialogue tailored to his voice and style.

Then arose the big question of who to cast opposite Jones. "It had to be an extraordinary, strong performer," says Parkes, "but a real contrast of styles and approaches to the world. Someone with great comic timing but who is also a real actor." They spent months talking about it, but as soon as Will Smith's name came up, "it was 'end of discussion.'" Sonnenfeld had wanted Smith ever since he himself joined the team, but the actor was too busy with his television show. Enough time elapsed before the film went into production, however, that Smith became available, right after finishing work on *Independence Day*. "So I got to have exactly the two actors I saw in the movie from the first time I read the script," says Sonnenfeld with satisfaction.

In working with the actors and their characters, Sonnenfeld took the approach that some of the most effective comedy can result when actors play it completely straight in an over-the-top situation. This was what he aimed for in *Men in Black*. "If you have a good script and you create an environment where the comedy is built in, then you don't have to try hard to be funny.

"Tommy Lee Jones turns out to be a comic genius in this style, as this picture reveals. Rip Torn and Linda Fiorentino can pull it off as well—they're really funny by doing almost nothing. So they all make good foils for Will, who of course is genuinely funny. He's the Deion Sanders of MIB agents."

Ed Solomon describes the process of fitting the lead actors into the script as comfortable and collaborative. Encouraged by Sonnenfeld, both Jones and Smith made suggestions for their dialogue—"with Tommy, it was usually cutting words, with Will more often adding a few," Solomon says. To the screenwriter this was a welcome indication that the actors were really inhabiting their characters. All the actors felt in good hands, working with some of the top production people in their business, which contributed to the generally easygoing atmosphere around the set. "It was a lot of fun to be on Barry's set," Tommy Lee Jones recalls, "very relaxed, very happy."

Agent Kay to the "pawnbroker" Jeebs: "You sold a carbonizer with implosion capacity to an unlicensed cephalopoid?" Tommy Lee Jones joined the *Men in Black* team long before the film went into production, and contributed significantly to script development.

Tommy Lee Jones ("Agent Kay")

Film veteran Tommy Lee Jones received his first Academy Award nomination in 1991 for his portrayal of Clay Shaw in Oliver Stone's *JFK*. Two years later, he won the Oscar for Best Supporting Actor and a Golden Globe Award for his performance as Marshall Gerard in the box-office hit *The Fugitive*.

Jones made his feature film debut in Arthur Hiller's *Love Story* (1970) as Ryan O'Neal's roommate. He has starred in more than 15 feature films including *Coal Miner's Daughter* (his first Golden Globe nomination), *Stormy Monday, Under Siege, Cobb, The Client, Natural Born Killers*, and *Blue Sky*. Most recently he starred as the notorious Harvey Two-Face in *Batman Forever*, and made his directorial debut on *The Good Old Boys* for TNT.

His television credits include *The Executioner's Song*, for which he won an Emmy portraying Gary Gilmore, as well as the title role in *The Amazing Howard Hughes*, an American Playhouse production of *Cat on a Hot Tin Roof*, and *The Rainmaker* for HBO. He was nominated for a Best Actor Emmy and a Golden Globe for the miniseries *Lonesome Dove*. He has won acclaim on the stage as well, with several Broadway roles to his credit.

One thing Jones hadn't done in his long and distinguished career was a science fiction film, and this was partly what motivated him to take on *Men in Black*. Aside from the potential for good adventure and chase scenes, the underlying questions raised by the story intrigued him: "Who or what is an alien? How do we relate to them? It's a relevant question for humans all around the world."

The other main attraction, he admits, was

***Above:* Agent Kay inspects a Noisy Cricket, a tiny weapon with a powerful punch. *Below:* The roles played by Tommy Lee Jones and Will Smith, as an older, worldly-wise agent and the up-and-coming rookie, closely parallel the current stages of their real-world careers.**

the background presence of Steven Spielberg. "To go into a large science fiction movie with a lot of special effects in it can be worrisome for an actor—unless the executive producer is Steven," he says, "in which case, you take a great deal of heart and confidence."

He also appreciated the chance to work with Sonnenfeld and Will Smith. "Barry's such a good cinematographer (his career before turning to directing), that we could be relaxed around the cameras." And he was happy to become a student in comedy with these two masters. "I'm playing the comedy precisely the way Barry tells me to, because he knows a lot about it and I don't know anything. I'm also happy to learn from Will, who is a very funny and generous young man."

Jones also sought and found a deeper side to his character in the screenplay. "It's the idea that we [the MIB] have to keep all this alien traffic through our little backwater border town of a planet secret from everyone else, because they couldn't handle the truth," he says. "I saw it as a great burden to go through life doing this kind of police work, knowing the truth that the rest of humanity doesn't know. It's a lonely life out there, and Kay's been living it for a long time. On one of the fenders of his black LTD there's a decal that reads 'K–2.' He's been with the Men in Black since the beginning."

An avid science fiction reader as a child, Jones currently professes no strong belief in extraterrestrial life or an agency like the MIB. But we're attracted to stories like this, he thinks, "because you would like to be able to suspect,

Before becoming a Man in Black, Will Smith, as New York City detective James Edwards, apprehends an alien perpetrator played by Keith Campbell.

or even hope, that there's life elsewhere. And that it's benevolent, it has things to teach us. I believe that hope is very real."

Will Smith ("Agent Jay")

Celebrated for his versatile talents in film, television, and music, Will Smith was most recently seen in the record-breaking summer hit *Independence Day*. That followed his starring role in *Bad Boys,* one of the biggest hits of 1995. His rising star was recognized when he was named Favorite Male Newcomer at the 1996 Blockbuster Awards.

A decade earlier, Smith burst onto the music scene as The Fresh Prince half of the Grammy-winning rap duo DJ Jazzy Jeff and The Fresh Prince. In 1992 the pair were honored at the NAACP Awards as Outstanding Rap Artists. Smith's charisma led to the creation of the NBC hit series *The Fresh Prince of Bel Air,* which recently completed its sixth season.

Smith's feature film work is highlighted by his acclaimed performance in the Oscar-nominated *Six Degrees of Separation.* Other credits include *Made in America,* and *Where the Day Takes You.*

Like his co-star, Will Smith names Steven Spielberg as a key reason why he joined the cast of *Men in Black*—and he describes how it happened in his inimitable comic style. "He called me and told me I had to do it. It was his baby. So it was like, okay, Steven Spielberg calls you, you're going to tell him, nah...I guess not."

Already well known from his television and music career, Smith's starring role in the 1996 blockbuster *Independence Day* brought him into Hollywood's top ranks. He admits to being mildly concerned about the prospect of following that immediately with another science fiction film, but points out that "they're two very different kinds of movies. *Independence Day* was more of a good old-fashioned disaster movie. This has more of a comedic edge."

In any case, he dove into his role with gusto, acquiring and reading all the *Men in Black* comics as well as the screenplay. He decided then and there that the MIB were very cool indeed. Smith has a dual role in a sense, in the film's early scenes playing the dedicated NYPD undercover detective Edwards, who takes his job very seriously.

"Jay is the kind of character who enjoys life," he says. "He enjoys experiencing new

Above: **Shooting the scene in which Agent Jay serves as midwife at the birth of a baby alien (here nestling on his lap).** ***Right:*** **The multitalented Smith shows his gifts for both comedy and action in** ***Men in Black.***

things. Also, he thinks he's the smartest person in the world, so this [becoming an MIB agent] is the ultimate challenge. Trying to adapt to that new world is what really drives this character—along with the same things that made him become a police officer: wanting to protect people and all that. The MIB is the ultimate police force."

Smith hugely enjoyed his partnership with Tommy Lee Jones, and the two play off each other brilliantly as the classic "old cop/new partner" team. He sees Jay and Kay's relationship as the younger agent trying to humanize the elder: "Jay thinks Kay is kind of grumpy.

Linda Fiorentino, best known for her award-winning performance in *The Last Seduction*, brings intelligence and intensity to her role as New York City medical examiner Dr. Laurel Weaver.

He understands that they have a job to do, but thinks they could enjoy it a little more. They don't have to be hard and rude, all those things that government guys usually are."

He also confesses to being slightly intimidated by Jones's reputation at first. "This is my fifth movie, and this guy's been making movies for thirty years plus. So I'm sitting there trying to make conversation, and Tommy Lee is telling me about the history of acting, and I'm like, yeah, so you hear the new Guru album? We don't have a lot of things in common—he's Tommy Lee Jones, you know, and I'm little Willy from Philly. But we had fun. Our differences are what brought us together."

Smith fell in completely with Barry Sonnenfeld's approach to the comedy. "What I love about the movie is, there's all this bizarre stuff going on—guys walking on the ceiling, aliens who look like worms or slugs—but you don't pay any attention to it. It's just part of the scene."

Linda Fiorentino ("Dr. Laurel Weaver")

Prior to *Men in Black,* Linda Fiorentino was best known for her work in the critically acclaimed erotic thriller *The Last Seduction,* for which she was named Best Actress by the New York Film Critics Circle. More recently she has starred in *Jade* and in John Dahl's *Unforgettable.*

Fiorentino made her feature film debut in Harold Becker's *Vision Quest* opposite Matthew Modine. She then portrayed a seductive SoHo sculptress in Martin Scorsese's *After Hours* and a runaway wife in Alan Rudolph's *The Moderns.* Her other films include *Gotcha!, Queens Logic,* and *Chain of Desire,* a remake of the classic *La Ronde.*

As Walter Parkes notes, the part of Dr. Weaver, though not large, is key to the story. "Her slightly offbeat quality was important" for her role as a somewhat spacey New York City coroner who—though she doesn't know it because the MIB have erased her memory so many times—has come into contact with more than a few aliens. "It was wonderful to get someone like Linda to come in and bring her strength to that character."

Fiorentino said she had no choice but to accept a part in a Barry Sonnenfeld-directed film, "because my stepson made me watch *Bad Boys* seven times. I also thought the script was very funny and handled rather uniquely, given the nature of the subject. The fact that's it's sci-fi but done with a comic touch. Basically, I think Tommy and I are around to make Will Smith seem even funnier."

Besides the need to play comedy, *Men in Black* posed another new challenge for Fiorentino: the action component. In the climactic scene when Laurel is taken hostage by the villain Edgar, "I was dragged around, kicked around, and thrown around; they put harnesses on me and I had to hang from a tree. And I did it all myself."

Vincent D'Onofrio ("Edgar")

Vincent D'Onofrio first came to prominence with his unforgettable performance as an unstable private in Stanley Kubrick's *Full Metal Jacket.* His other films include *Strange Days, Ed Wood, Being Human, The Player, JFK, Adventures in Babysitting,* and *Mystic Pizza.* He was most recently seen in *Feeling Minnesota* with Keanu

Actor Vincent D'Onofrio in full make-up for his role as Edgar, the evil insectoid alien who uncomfortably inhabits a human skin.

Reeves, *The Whole Wide World* (which he produced), and Alex Cox's recently released *The Winner.*

The Brooklyn-born D'Onofrio has appeared on Broadway in *Of Mice and Men, Sexual Perversity in Chicago,* and *The Indian Wants the Bronx*. He studied acting at the American Stanislavsky Theatre and the Actors Studio in New York.

D'Onofrio's method acting skills were formidably tested in *Men in Black,* where he plays a merciless insectoid space alien who moves around on Earth in the body of a human named Edgar. The premise is that this eight-foot-tall insect somehow compresses himself, cocoon-like, into a human skin. The actor's take on the situation is that being stuffed into this body not only makes the Edgar character move strangely, but provokes serious frustration. "His mannerisms and speech patterns are very bizarre, because there's this thing inside him that's moving around.

"We're doing a kind of villain that hasn't been done before, in that he veers from being completely scary to just odd or darkly funny. It's hard to play that—to be funny and evil at the same time. I'm trying to incorporate this in everything he does: the way he speaks, the way he moves, his whole manner. Hopefully it will be interesting and unique."

D'Onofrio spent most of his time on the MIB set in a make-up chair, to achieve the horrible effect that he was literally wearing someone else's skin. There were several different versions, or stages, of this special make-up, to suggest that the "host skin" was progressively decomposing over the course of the film. To apply the make-up completely took upwards of six hours, which D'Onofrio spent in the trailer with make-up chief Rick Baker and his appliance specialist David Anderson.

The actor had worked with Baker on an earlier film, in fact, and prior to shooting the two collaborated for several months to develop the Edgar make-up. "Both those guys are incredible artists. Hanging out with them every day, for as long as we had to, brought us pretty close together. The make-up itself was not fun; it was actually painful at times. But our interac-

***Above:* Special effects make-up artist Rick Baker works on Vincent D'Onofrio. *Below:* Veteran actor Rip Torn plays Agent Zed, the MIB headquarters chief, in a straight performance with comic undertones.**

Above: **A small but key role in the film is that of Beatrice, the beleaguered, then liberated, wife of the redneck Edgar, whose body is usurped by the bug alien. She's portrayed by Siobhan Fallon.** ***Right:*** **Carl Striken as an Arquillian diplomat who visits Earth to negotiate for a disputed galaxy.** ***Below:*** **Tony Shaloub as Jeebs, the alien turned pawnbroker.**

tion was fun—it can be a six-hour conversation sometimes."

In the last two years, D'Onofrio has also produced two of his own films, on the limited resources standard for such indie projects. It's given him a whole new respect for the challenges involved in a project on the much vaster scale of *Men in Black*. "The second unit crew on this film was bigger than our first unit. So it's a completely different world—they're both as interesting as the other."

Director Sonnenfeld gives high marks to his supporting cast, noting how well Rip Torn as Zed fell into the deadpan style of comedy, and also singling out performances by Tony Shaloub as the pawnbroker Jeebs and Carl Striken (who played Lurch in Sonnenfeld's Addams Family pictures) as the alien Arquillian diplomat. All the actors, for their part, give Sonnenfeld high marks not only for his efficient masterminding of the complex production, but the loose, relaxed atmosphere he cultivated. "He's very funny himself," comments Linda Fiorentino, "and he really energizes a set."

But of all the players seen on the screen, the one who may have most thoroughly enjoyed the experience is comic book creator Lowell Cunningham—even though his moment of glory will likely be missed by audiences. Cunningham, who spent several days on the set as consultant, appears briefly as a nerdy short-sleeved support agent in the background of a scene at the Men in Black headquarters.

He recalls his first encounter with filming as the most exciting. "I arrived when they were shooting the opening scene on the border, and Tommy Lee Jones was there. It was tremendously exciting to see a big star playing one of my characters. And the big black car was in the shot too—so it was all amazingly similar to my first glimpse of the MIB legend in real life."

RICK BAKER AND HIS ALIENS

"I can make toys and play with them...really cool toys."
—*Rick Baker*

PRIOR TO THE START of production, the filmmakers began collaborating with special make-up effects artist Rick Baker in the spring of 1995. For more than a year, Baker and his colleagues at Cinovation worked to design and create a host of alien creatures to populate *Men in Black*. Baker also executed the special make-up needed to transform actor Vincent D'Onofrio into the character of Edgar.

Included in the menagerie are body-suit performers and fully automated creatures guided by the skillful hands and voices of more than thirty puppeteers who have worked extensively on projects like *Babe, The Muppet Show,* and *Short Circuit.* Baker's creations in conjunction with Industrial Light & Magic's visual effects have been integrated seamlessly into the carefully designed world of *Men in Black*.

Rick Baker has been nominated five times and won four Academy Awards for his work in the films *Ed Wood, Harry and the Hendersons, An American Werewolf in London,* and most recently *The Nutty Professorr,* starring Eddie Murphy. In addition to being nominated for an Academy Award, he also received a BAFTA Award for *Greystoke: The Legend of Tarzan, Lord of the Apes.* His other films include *Just Cause, Batman Forever, Wolf, The Rocketeer, Gorillas in the Mist, Coming to America, Starman, Star Wars* (the cantina sequence), and *King Kong.*

Special effects make-up artist Rick Baker peers into the head of a human robot at the tiny, animated "little green man" alien created by his team.

"I was a weird kid. I liked monster movies and stuff. I was one of the first generations of kids to grow up on TV, and I was drawn to the kind of films that used special effects. As a real little kid, I thought I wanted to be a doctor—which my mother was all excited about. But later it came to me that the only reason I wanted to be a doctor was because of Frankenstein."

—*Rick Baker*

"Working on *Men in Black* was a lot of fun," says Baker, "partly because it utilized almost everything we do here. It was make-up and animatronic stuff. We had guys in body-suits; we had little bitty puppets; we had big mechanical things. Some of it was high-tech and some was very low-tech. We had just about every kind of thing we can make here at Cinovation, all rolled up into one film."

Producer Walter Parkes notes that Amblin had a congenial long-term relationship with Baker, going back to *Gremlins.* "His stuff is not

Above: When the alien Mikey sheds his human disguise, his human head, which he holds on a pole, keeps talking. This unsettling effect was produced by combining live-action footage of a model head and computer graphics technology. _Below:_ A Cinovation artist puts finishing touches on the "Baby Redgick" puppet.

just imaginative but really witty—there's a spin on all of it, a great sense of humor operating in his work. And on top of all that, he makes creatures that actually work. Both were absolutely essential for this film."

Barry Sonnenfeld concurs. "You always want Rick because he's the best at this in the world. And you never think you can get him. We considered other collaborators, but my theory is; go with the best and it'll end up being cheapest because it'll look really good and you won't have to do it again." It was not at all certain that Baker could be had for *Men in Black*,

"I especially like the squid guy (an alien that floats in a tank) because if there are aliens, they probably don't have two arms, two legs, and two eyes like us. In fact, there's probably one here right now that we're not seeing because it looks just like air. So we wanted to avoid as much as possible just having guys in funny suits."

—Barry Sonnenfeld

since he was still busy with *The Nutty Professor* ("seventy days of making up Eddie Murphy") when work started. By the time he could come on board, the film was well into pre-production, and Baker had to get busy and create a whole array of creatures in a short time.

New to the sci-fi genre, Barry Sonnenfeld brought few specific ideas about what *Men in Black's* aliens should look like. Nor did the script give many clues, beyond descriptions like "a giant space bastard." The fact that they weren't a single race of aliens from a single planet—the story permitted aliens from all over

Opposite: A pair of "capacious cranium" aliens tends to the squid alien in its special tank at MIB Headquarters. *Above:* A Cinovation sculptor works on a small-scale clay model of the Edgar Bug's head. *Below:* Bobo the Squat is among the film's several aliens portrayed by body-suit performers.

the universe to come to Earth—gave Baker and his crew virtually carte blanche to let their imaginations and talents run wild.

"Time was short, so we just started doing designs—tons of designs," Baker recalls. "We couldn't just do anything we wanted—there was Barry and Steven and others who had to approve things—but we just kept throwing ideas at them until we ran out of time for changes and had to commit to some designs."

Even so, things changed even during production. "The worm guys, for example, was an early idea that had been rejected—really just a test to play with some rod-puppets. But later on, Barry wanted to add more aliens, so we brought them out again and he said 'perfect'. And it was my suggestion to add the passport control center for the aliens to the MIB headquarters set—partly as a way to show a bunch of aliens lined up together, and to explain how they get their disguises."

Mindful of the filmmakers' emphasis on character more than special effects, Baker and his crew imbued all the aliens—from the amphibious Mikey of the border scene to the "little green man" known as Mr. Gentle—with distinct personalities. It's a direction that comes naturally to him.

"What I like is making characters," he states. "I don't really like the blood and gore things as much as creating creatures with personality." Having said that, he also admits to having great fun conceiving the fearsome, scaly 12-foot-tall "bugmeister" that bursts out of Edgar's skin at the movie's climax.

Baker started out as a conventional make-up artist, but with the growth of special effects technology and movies involving aliens—spurred by the *Star Wars* trilogy and *Close Encounters of the Third Kind*—he soon gained an unmatched reputation as a "creature creator." His company, Cinovation, now employs 70 people and contracts with specialists in puppetry and other fields. Their work spans the effects spectrum, low-tech to high: from prosthetic make-up to simple hand or rod puppets, body-suit performers to mechanical or electronically animated creatures.

Increasingly they collaborate with CGI technicians such as those at Industrial Light & Magic to help animate their creations in previ-

Making "Mr. Gentle"

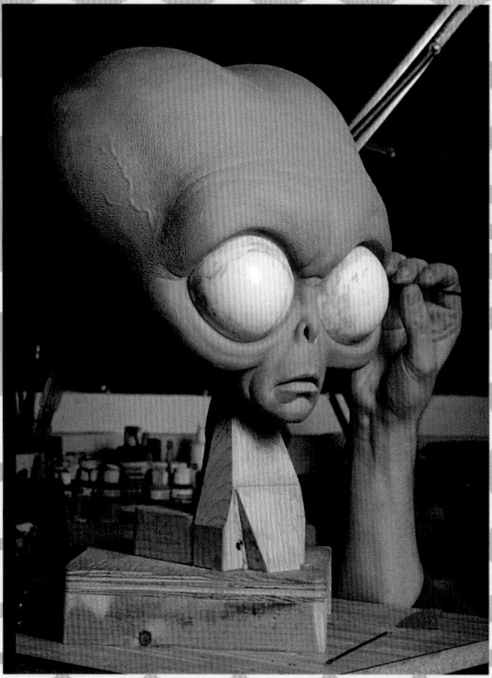

One of *Men in Black's* memorable aliens appears briefly but is key to the plot, and makes a big emotional impact. This is "the Baltian prince," known on the set as "the little green man" or "Mr. Gentle." Just a few inches high, he exists on Earth inside the head of a human robot (played by Mike Nussbaum), masquerading as an elderly jeweler. The "jeweler" keeps a beloved pet cat, around whose neck hangs a pretty charm—in reality, an entire galaxy over which the Baltians and Arquillians have warred for centuries. We see the Baltian only when the head of his host robot is opened in the city morgue, revealing the alien prince operating the controls as he is dying.

To create this remarkable image, Rick Baker and his colleagues actually made two "green men." One was a tiny life-size model to be photographed inside the robot's head—"the smallest thing we've done," says Baker. But in order for Mr. Gentle to speak, blink his eyes, change expressions, and manipulate his joysticks, they also had to make a larger-scale figure, about 12 feet tall. A complicated mechanism of servo-motors controlled these fine movements.

The robot head itself was a big project, requiring molds, sculpting, airbrushing, implanting individual hairs, and building in a mechanism to make vapor come out of its ears.

"It's one of those cases where an incredible amount of work goes into a few seconds of screen time," notes Baker. But according to Will Smith, it was worth it. "I was really fond of that little green man," says the actor wistfully. "I was sad when he died."

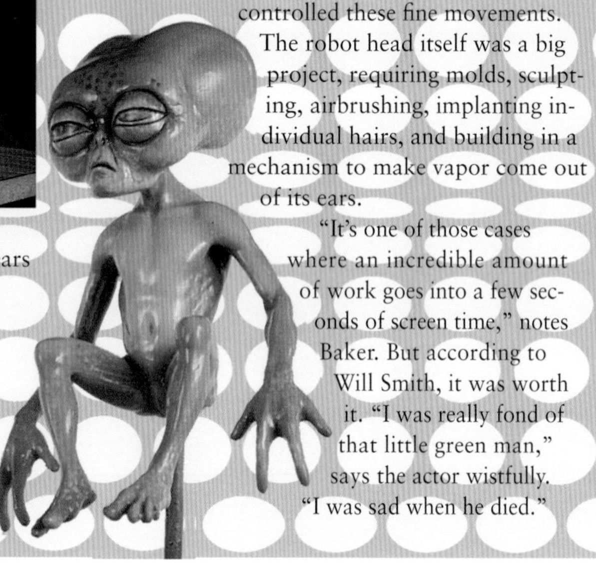

ously undreamed-of ways. "But I am still very hands on" Baker says. "If it was up to me, I'd like to design and sculpt all day."

That's impossible, given the scale of his operation, but Baker does remain hands-on when it comes to special face and body makeup like Eddie Murphy's in *The Nutty Professor,* or Vincent D'Onofrio's in *Men in Black*. "In the end, working with Vincent was probably my favorite part of the film. He was incredibly patient and tolerant of the terrible things we did to him, and we've become good friends."

Tony Shaloub plays Jeebs the pawnbroker, whose head is shot off and regenerated in one scene. The effect involved detailed collaboration between Cinovation and ILM; Shaloub describes his own behind-the-scenes work: "For the scene where Jeebs regenerates his head, I had to spend some time at Rick Baker's shop. First they took a life cast of my head and shoulders, completely covered in plaster, so they could make a mold of

***Above:* An artist works on the large model of "Mr. Gentle," and a finished sculpture of the miniature model, shown just slightly smaller than actual size. *Opposite:* Rick Baker and his crew send Mavis 12 and Mavis 13 before the camera; small-stature actors play these aliens.**

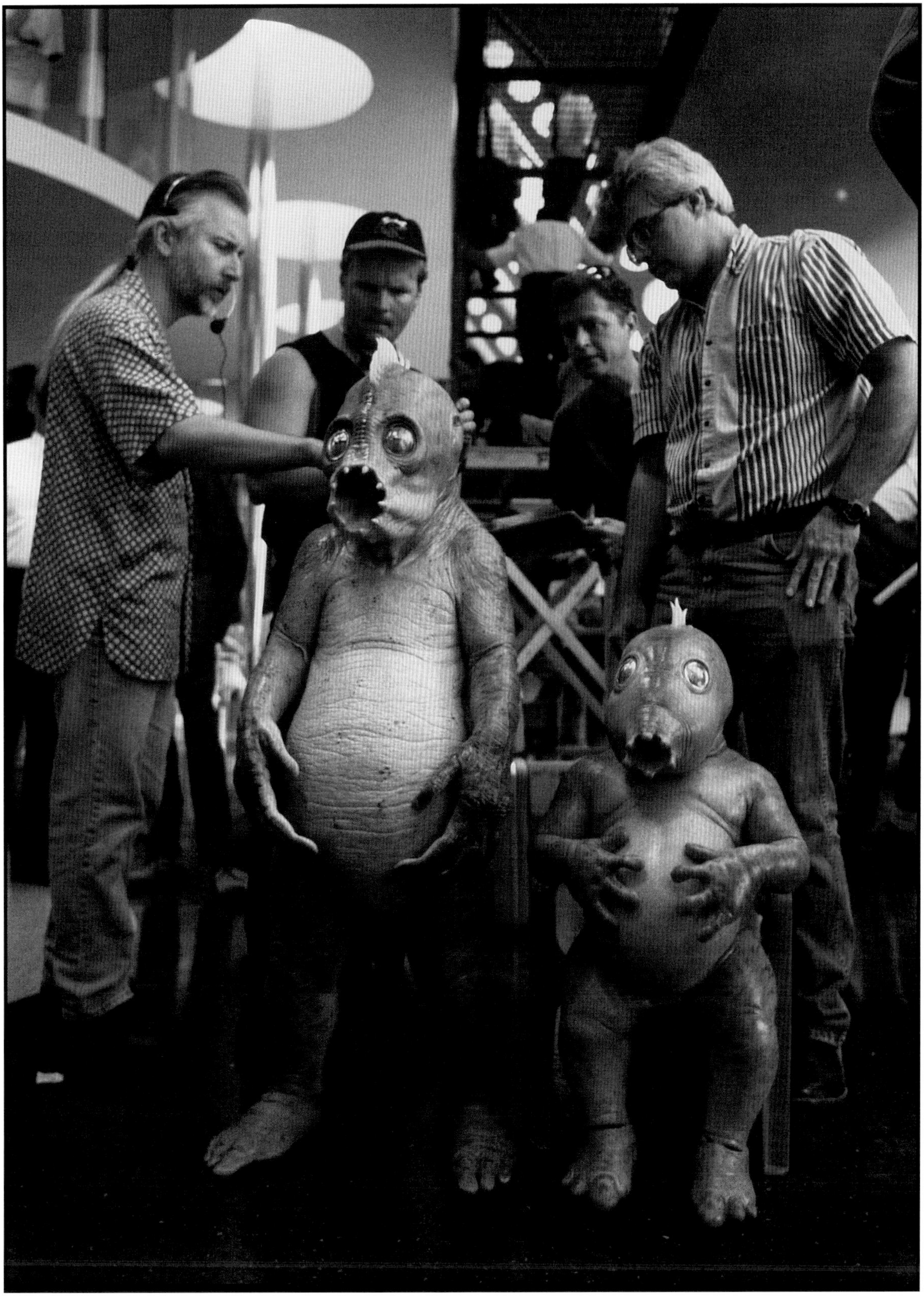

"I thought the Edgar bug needed to be really big and scary, because Tommy Lee Jones and Will Smith are so forceful and charismatic, you need a really good villain to play against them."

—Barry Sonnenfeld

my head. Then I had to do an entire body cast, which is frightening. You stand up and they wrap you like a mummy, right up to your neck, and let the stuff harden. I was thinking: this is Los Angeles, what if there's an earthquake right now? These guys are going to just scatter and leave me here, locked in stone. Of course that didn't happen, but it was still an unsettling experience."

Baker tries not to dwell on the fact that his creations, which can take months of painstaking work, may appear on the screen for only a few seconds. "Hopefully a really cool few seconds." He's clearly a man in love with what he does, and plans to keep on doing it. "I've been offered chances to direct, and I think I'm just about the only person in Hollywood who doesn't want to. I used to make my own 8mm movies and that was fun, but running a big production like this takes so much out of people. I like being able to focus on what I do, and I like knowing I had a big part in what people will see in this movie. There are a lot of entertaining things to look at."

THE TRANSFORMERS—PUTTING IT ALL TOGETHER AT ILM

CONSISTENT WITH ALL THEIR EFFORTS to bring the film industry's best talent to bear on *Men in Black*, Columbia and Amblin engaged the northern California firm of Industrial Light & Magic to craft special visual effects for the film. The ILM team was involved from the earliest stages of pre-production and was an integral part of conceiving the visual style of *Men in Black*. Their work in the post-production phase put the final polish on the creature and mechanical effects designed by Rick Baker, and literally stitched the film together shot by shot.

"There are a lot of people doing amazing visual effects," comments Walter Parkes, "but for 3D character animation, where you're actually creating an artifact that only exists in a computer and giving it absolutely natural motion, I don't think anyone's been able to pull that off to the extent ILM can. They were the

Opposite: **Jay faces off with the full-size Edgar Bug.** ***Above:*** **An effects shot of the bug spewing goo at the MIB.** ***Below:*** **Left to right, director Barry Sonnenfeld, first assistant director Ed Hirsch, visual effects supervisor Eric Brevig, computer graphics supervisor Carl Frederick, and animation supervisor Rob Coleman, review dailies.**

The ILM stage crew rigs a miniature flying saucer for filming the sequence in which it crashes through the World's Fair Unisphere, also shown in scale model. *Inset:* The fiery moment of impact, a pyrotechnics effect.

ones who could bring the kind of real, breathing life into these creatures that we wanted."

Overseeing the work of a large team of effects specialists was visual effects supervisor Eric Brevig, who also served as second unit director. Brevig, who won an Academy Award for his fx work on Arnold Schwarzenegger's *Total Recall,* echoes Rick Baker when he points to the great variety of effects used as the film's greatest challenge and most interesting aspect for him. "Most films that rely on effects tend use a single type of effect throughout, but here we've got all kinds. We have animated creatures, flying saucers, state-of-the-art computer-generated monsters, and something that looks like a 50s sci-fi movie scene, all in one project."

Men in Black is also extraordinary in the sheer number of shots that incorporate special effects: somewhere in the neighborhood of 250. Compare this with 60 for *Jurassic Park,* or around 190 for its sequel *The Lost World,* in the works at ILM concurrently with *Men in Black*. In all, the ILM team devoted one year to the task of meticulously crafting all these shots, says visual effects producer Jacqui Lopez.

ILM is acknowledged as the industry's premier source of visual effects technology, in part because they can do it all. Their staff of experts includes modelmakers, painters, animators, effects supervisors, and developers of proprietary software for some of their in-computer work. They can build and photograph miniature sets, create and animate creatures in the computer, and composite the footage they generate with live-action footage from the first-unit shoot, through the miracle of technology and talent.

When ILM comes onto a project like *Men in Black,* work begins in pre-production with meetings between Brevig, Lopez, and the director and producer to talk through the script. During production, Brevig is on the first-unit set nearly every day to supervise members of the computer graphics crew. While there, they must gather dozens of details that allow them to precisely integrate the digital effects with the live-action photography into a seamless final image. These details include measuring the size and angle and topography of every element on the set. Brevig is also available to help the filmmakers sort out technical problems and advise where difficulties can be resolved in post-production. Based on information he provides, technicians back at ILM create 3D computer grids of each set, so that animated figures can be placed accurately.

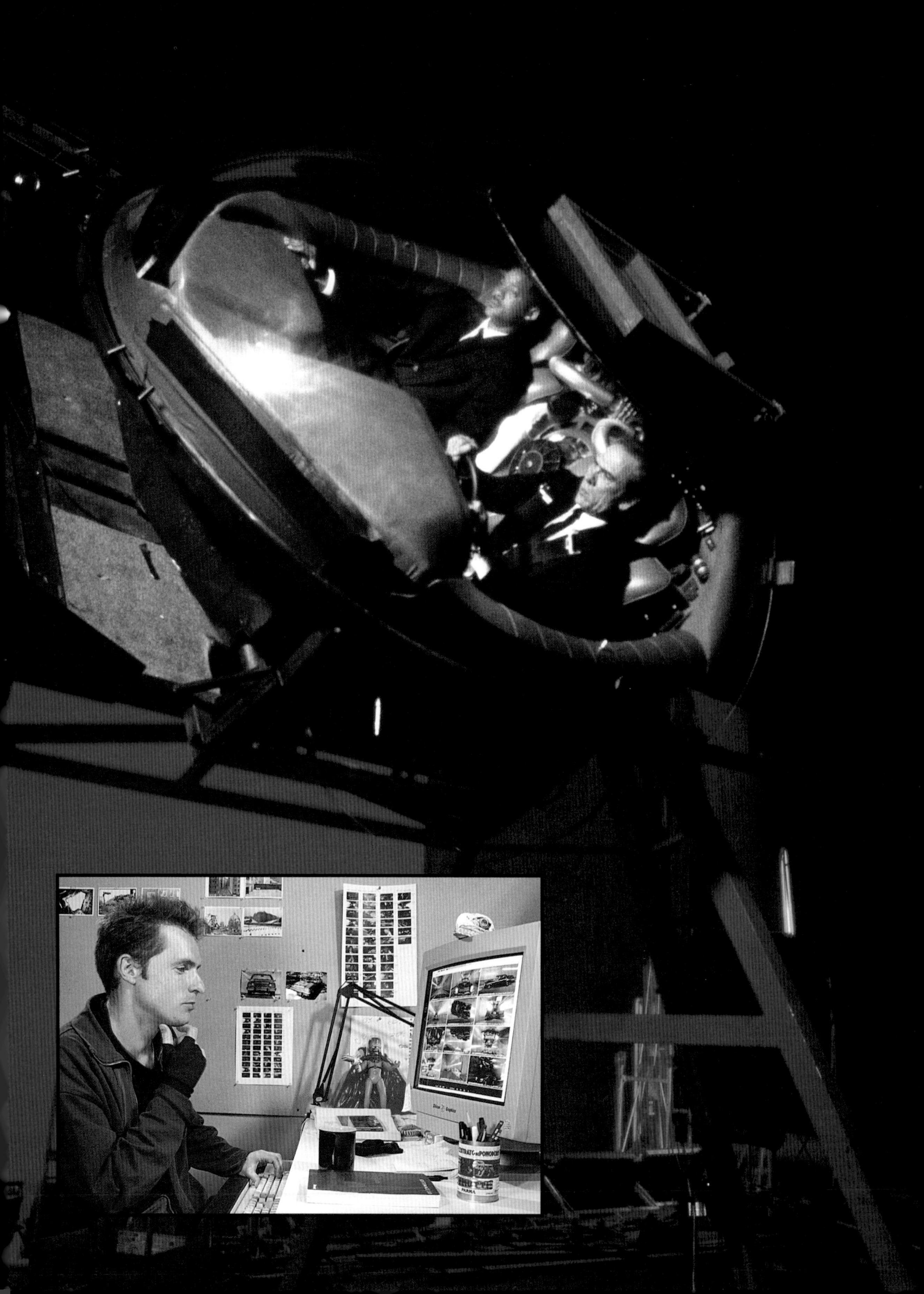

A visit to ILM's headquarters while work on *Men in Black* is in full swing reveals the full scope of the endeavor. In one cavernous space, camera operators and modelmakers hover over a 96-foot-long replica of a stretch of New York's Queens Midtown Tunnel, through which agents Kay and Jay race upside-down in their airborne supercar, fantastically transformed from a prosaic Ford LTD. The model, exactly eight times smaller than the real tunnel, is authentic down to its graffiti, dingy fluorescent lights, and oil-slicked pavement. The "traffic" photographed in it is an array of finely detailed model cars—mostly cabs, plus a few vans, sedans, muscle cars, and a slat-side truck hauling a tricked-out Harley. All have working head- and tail-lights, and are occupied by tiny drivers and passengers.

Opposite: In front of the bluescreen, Tommy Lee Jones and Will Smith pilot the car module that simulates a gravity-defying dash through the Midtown Tunnel. _Inset:_ ILM technical director Gerald Gutschmidt manipulates computer graphics to complete the car effect. _Right:_ Pat Sweeney, visual effects director of photography, sets up the motion control camera in the model tunnel. _Below:_ The final effect of the transformed car in motion.

Above: **The ILM crew films stars Jones and Smith at ILM for the bluescreen portion of the saucer crash. Technicians use air blowers to mimic the impact of the crash nearly at their feet.** ***Opposite:*** **The alien Mikey being helped into costume.**

The tunnel set-up took four months to build and photograph, and all this work will boil down to about 90 seconds of screen time. It's simply part of the game, says visual effects director of photography Pat Sweeney. The level of detail needed to produce "a reality that works on the screen" requires an extremely time-consuming and precise technique called motion control photography. Sweeney's team will shoot video tests in the tunnel to work out any bugs, then shoot final film utilizing this motion control technique. It's an intricate process in which a camera on an overhead track passes slowly along its length, as technicians consecutively raise and lower hinged sections of the tunnel roof to allow the camera arm to pass through. Later, this film will be composited with shots of Kay and Jay in a CGI version of the transformed car.

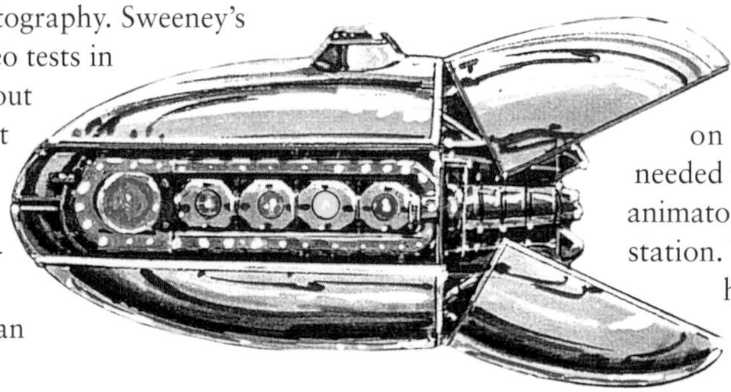

In dramatic contrast to this big model set-up occupying 5,000 square feet of floor space, another vital part of the work goes on in the compact space needed to house a computer animator and his or her workstation. These folks are the heartbeat of ILM's awesome reputation for

Bringing Creatures to Life

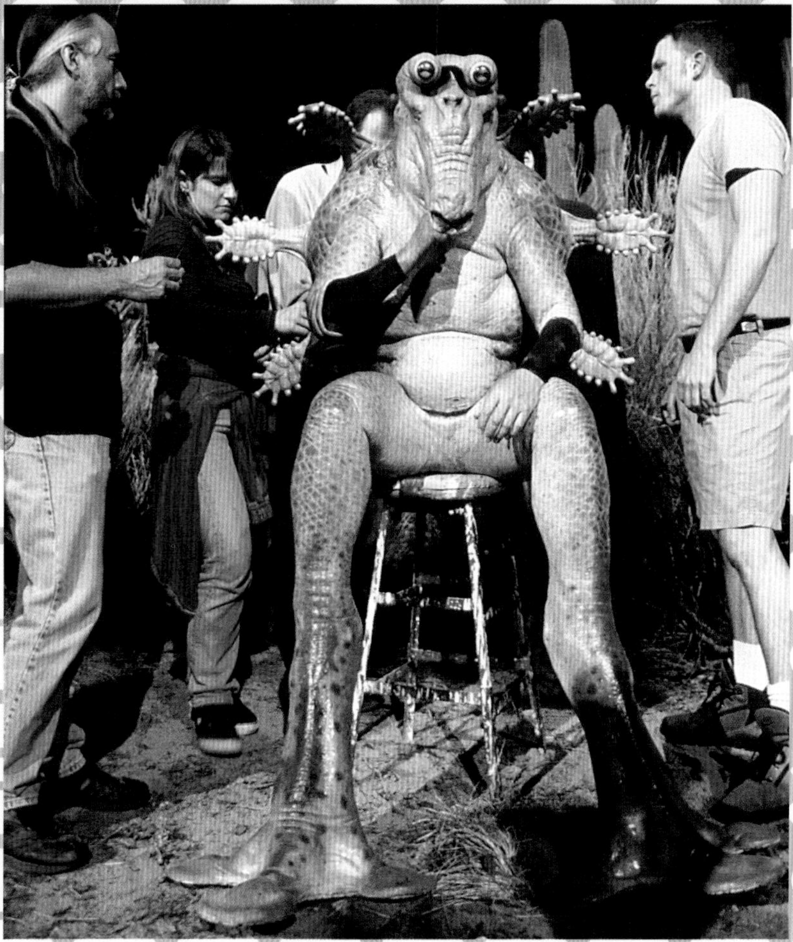

In creating *Men in Black*'s aliens, the ILM team worked closely with Rick Baker and Cinovation. "In many cases we're taking Rick's designs and creating computer-generated versions of those creatures," says Eric Brevig. "Often these days you'll have an actual puppet (or body-suit performer) that works great for closeups or specific actions but can't move or run around in all the ways desired. Or it may be impossible to block out the rods, wires, puppeteer, or other mechanics. So to perfect the performance we create a computer version of the same figure, painstakingly animated in post-production, which can be made to do just about anything you want."

An example of how live action and 3D CGI animation are interwoven in *Men in Black* is the alien Mikey (disguised as a human in the opening scene). In the first reveal, we are seeing the computer-generated version, because Mikey has to hunch down in a tight space—tough on an actor in a bulky latex suit. In the next view, the body-suit Mikey is seen in dialogue with Tommy Lee Jones; it's live action. Finally, when Mikey attacks and is blown to bits, again it's the CGI creature we see.

movie magic. Using proprietary software developed by the company, they can create anything from a microscopic image to a galaxy, and bring it to life on the screen.

When working with 3D CGI—creature animation or morphing humanoids, for example—they start at the skeletal level, programming in incredibly detailed parameters for size, shape, and range of motion. Then they build up the figure from the inside out, digitally imposing natural physics on the muscular system, the fat layer, and finally the skin. "Getting a natural look for eyes, mouths, and lips is especially tricky," notes Eric Brevig. "Surface texture and the degree of reflectivity can make a huge difference in the believability of the results."

In still another part of ILM's warren of offices and warehouses, an entire project team settles down to review the morning's dailies under the supervision of a technical director. (The process is so complex that each shot has its own technical director!) As an operator at a computer console selects any sequence in progress, the TD, animators, painters, and other team members minutely critique the composition, framing, color, animation quality, level of realism, and timing of shot moves, almost frame by frame.

In one sequence, the giant Edgar bug is blown to smithereens, and as the tape rolls forward and back, a stunt double flies time after time out of the creature's stomach. The quantity and range of "blue goo" being sprayed around, the trajectory of the stunt double, the framing and lighting of the whole scene, are all dissected at length. As another shot is reviewed, the blown-off head of Jeebs (an alien disguised as a pawnbroker) regenerates again and again. The animator admits that the head bears a distinct resemblance to that archetypal alien known as E.T.—"a brief homage to the executive producer."

A sci-fi/action movie like *Men in Black* calls upon the whole range of special effects available. (See the sidebar on different kinds of effects.) Mechanical special effects designer Peter Chesney is in charge of all the elements related to the film's physical world—as opposed to visual or optical effects done in the computer or the camera. In practice, this often centers on "explosions and pyrotechnics."

A special challenge in *Men in Black* was the scene where Will Smith chases Edgar through the streets of New York while shooting his "Noisy Cricket"—a tiny gun that packs a big punch. Chesney somehow had to create the effect of powerful explosions on location in a quiet Greenwich Village neighborhood, where residents were understandably leery. "We did lots of preliminary testing at a fire department training center," says Chesney, working their way down to where the blast looks big but really isn't. "It's a lot easier just to do a big fireball and chew up the vehicle. But this one's surgically calibrated so that nobody has a rattled window or a shook-up kittycat."

The filmmakers also wanted a "green alien laser de-atomizer" effect, to suggest the far-out nature of the weapons used by the MIB. In one case, says Chesney, this was achieved with something as mundane as "little Dixie Cups full of

glittery stars." The blue flare guns used to shoot down Edgar's spaceship needed a more elaborate effort. "We actually used five or six components, plus special 'reactive lighting' to show the result of the blast. It would have been hard to do optically because you can't control lighting on actors' faces as well." The final ingredients in this witch's brew were a combination of highly pressurized alcohol and copper sulfate, producing a solution that glowed bright blue. This was supplemented with high-pressure nitrogen to drive it, argon CO2 purge gas "to keep some little fires happening," and electric solenoids to make the guns light up.

And then there was the infamous "blue goo," liberally sprayed around whenever an alien was blasted. Among other innovations for *Men in Black*, says Chesney, "We've pioneered some new, interesting slime."

Opposite and above: **The end of the saucer crash sequence, as created on site and in the ILM computers: after smashing through the Unisphere, the ship lands hard on the grounds of the World's Fair.** ***Below:*** **First assistant director Ed Hirsch, visual effects producer Jacqui Lopez, and Eric Brevig (right) watch footage of the sequence on a monitor.**

The Language of Special Effects

Within the world of movie special effects, there are several different categories:

Physical effects	Also sometimes called simply "special effects." Usually created during production, often by the second-unit. Includes mechanical and practical effects.
Practical effects	Explosions and pyro
Mechanical effects	May include fireworks, but also any effect produced by mechanical means: hydraulics, electric motors, etc.
Visual effects	Usually finished in post-production. Taking what is photographed and augmenting it in some way. Formerly done with camera trickery (and called in-camera effects), now more often with computers.
Optical effects	Before computers, effects achieved with optical compositing equipment that used projection techniques in combining different pieces of film.
CGI	Computer-generated imaging: the process pioneered by ILM of creating visual effects digitally—whether backgrounds, environments, or characters.
Motion control photography	A filming process in which a camera's motions are controlled precisely by a computer, allowing for repeated filmings (developed originally for *Star Wars*).

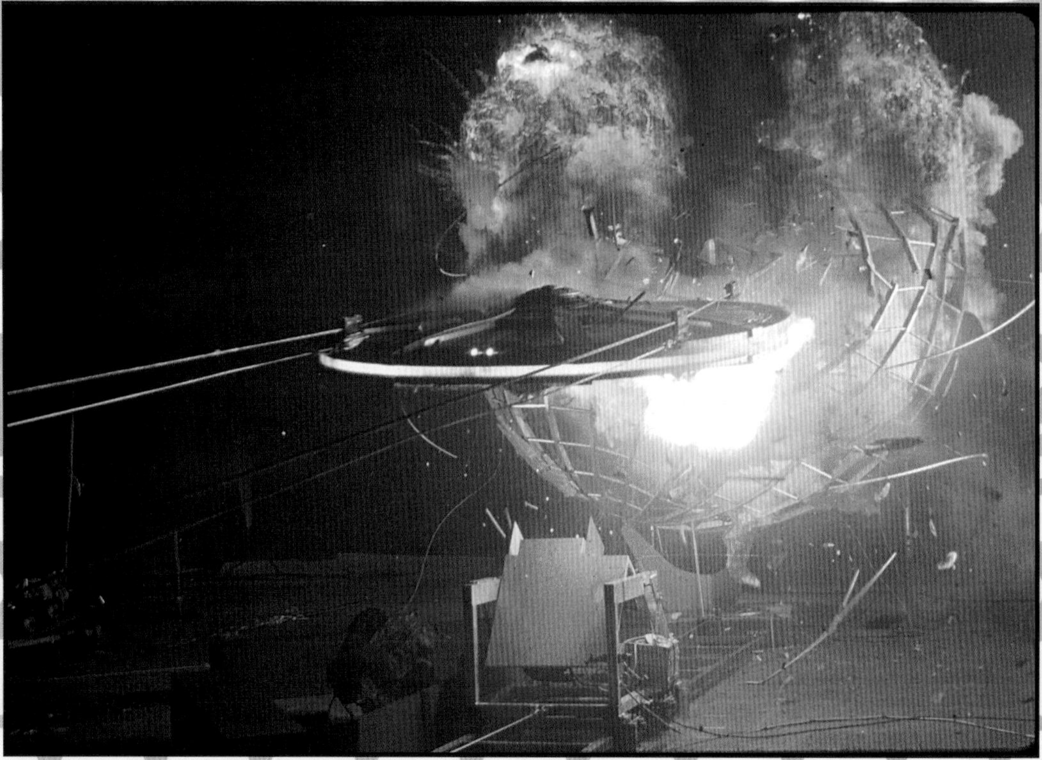

Our fascination with the possibility of extraterrestrial life, and our fears that "someone" may not want us to know about such things, have been part of our consciousness for the last half-century. *Men in Black* comes along at a time when movies and television are exploiting this interest as never before: we need only name *Independence Day, Mars Attack!*, and *The X-Files* to illustrate the trend. As it happened, *Men in Black* had been scripted long before any of these were released, though its long gestation period caused it to make a later appearance.

Comic book creator Lowell Cunningham shares some background on his inspiration for *Men in Black:* "The concept is often compared

Right: An INS agent winds up covered with "blue goo" when Mikey is blasted. _Below:_ The next time you sit near a couple of strange-looking guys in a deli, look again. These two are a Baltian prince [in a robot body] and an Arquillian, both from worlds many light years from Earth.

with *The X-Files,* though it was around long before that show." Both Chris Carter, who created *The X-Files,* and Cunningham have mentioned the 1970s Darren McGavin series *The Night Stalker* as an influence—they grew up watching that as well as early spy programs. But whereas Carter seems to have mixed elements of that show with aspects of the old *FBI* series (starring Efrem Zimbalist, Jr.), "I was probably influenced more by *The Man From UNCLE*—with its humorous approach and two main characters in suits—in coming up with MIB."

Cunningham is happy to note that Marvel Comics will release a new series of *Men in Black* comics this summer, to coincide with the film's release. Sony's licensing department is making sure that MIB toys and other merchandise tie-ins will be part of the big picture, and the Warner Brothers TV channel will premiere an animated *Men in Black* series, to air in a prime Saturday daytime slot right after *Superman.*

But the feature film is still the main event, and the makers of *Men in Black* have gone to great lengths to make sure it works on every level they intended. Audiences who love exciting action, aliens (cute and cuddly or scaly and scary), impressive pyrotechnics, transforming vehicles, and suspenseful chases won't be disappointed.

But it was important from the start—to Steven Spielberg, Walter Parkes and Laurie MacDonald, and certainly to Barry Sonnenfeld—that the movie go several steps further, to engage viewers with the fate of its characters and gently urge them to think about some larger questions. Says Sonnenfeld:

"It's a really big film that's going to look like a small, intimate romance in some ways. I want it to feel real, so it's not going to look like a lot of other effects movies: all noise and colors and explosions.

"Even though it's a huge production and we have plenty of aliens, ultimately it's about the script and the characters. All the effects and creatures are very entertaining—but if you don't pay attention to the story and the actors, no one's going to care about the movie. We have a great story and wonderful actors, and that's really why people go to the movies. "

The spacecraft commandeered from the World's Fair site by the Edgar Bug looms over nearby Shea Stadium. Just another evening in New York....

MEN IN BLACK
Official Agent's Manual

You'll conform to the identify we give you.

You will have no identifying marks of any kind.

You will not stand out in any way.

Your entire image is crafted to leave no lasting memory.

You're a rumor, recognizable only as déja vu.

You don't exist; you were never born.

Anonymity is your name.

Silence is your native tongue.

You are no longer part of the system.

We're above the system. Over it. Beyond it.

We are the Men in Black.

MIB
MEN IN BLACK

MIB
MEN IN BLACK

Men in Black Is an Equal Opportunity Employer

Dear New Recruit:

Congratulations. You have been chosen to join the most important law enforcement team on earth. For more than thirty years, the Men in Black (MIB) have monitored alien activity on Earth, provided intergalactic immigrations services, and represented the planet Earth in fifth-dimension foreign affairs.

Your job is to investigate any and all unlawful acts committed by aliens. In addition to the laws specifically outlined in this Manual (see Alien Penal Codes, page 75), space creatures are expected to abide by all the same laws as U.S. citizens—except jaywalking. (Our feeling is, cross at your own risk.) See to it that these laws are strictly observed.

The use of physical force against aliens should be considered a last resort. Intergalactic law mandates that nonviolent negotiation tactics be employed before forcibly subduing a space criminal. But, in the end, we expect you to use whatever means are necessary to keep the planet safe.

It is also imperative that all MIB investigations remain a secret. In 1967 the United Intergalactic Community (UIC) unanimously decided that because humans are "too stupid for their own good" it is advisable to keep alien activity confidential.

Your role as an MIB agent should not be taken lightly. The safety of the planet rests in your hands. Every man, woman, child—not to mention cat and dog—depends on you. There can be no life, liberty and pursuit of happiness without the Men in Black.

That is all. Good luck, and Godspeed.

Sincerely,

May
Director of Human Resources

504 Battery Drive, New York, New York 10000 • Telephone unlisted; we'll call you

IDENTITY RELEASE FORM FOR NEW AGENTS

I ______________________________ , being of sound mind and body, do hereby
(state your name)

irrevocably terminate all rights to my current identity. I understand that all personal documents—including birth certificate, driver's license, and social security number—will be expunged from the record. I also agree to have my fingerprints extinguished. I recognize that this procedure may be painful, but that once commenced, it cannot be aborted. This document supersedes and revokes all prior claims to said identity.

This declaration is made on this __________ day of __________ , 19_______.
date month year

__________________________ __________________________ ,
Declarant witness

residing at ____
address

MIB
NOTARY

Kate Kradutz

FIELD PLACEMENT EVALUATION

The following survey will help us determine where you would best serve the MIB. Complete this form using a number two pencil.

Choose the best answer for the following question.

1. If spacecraft A is traveling due west at 30 times the speed of light, and spacecraft B is traveling due east at 40 times the speed of light, at what point will the two spacecrafts collide?
   a. when the moon is in the seventh house.
   b. when Jupiter aligns with Mars.
   c. when peace will guide the planet, and love will rule the stars.
   d. never, because spacecraft A's flight was canceled.

2. I am ________ with zero gravity.
   a. very comfortable
   b. somewhat comfortable
   c. not at all comfortable

3. I __________ travel(ing) at speeds in excess of 5 million miles an hour.
   a. enjoy
   b. don't mind
   c. would rather be stuck in traffic for 6 hours than

4. Which of the following adverse conditions sounds least appealing?
   a. being trapped on a planet where surface temperatures exceed 300 degrees.
   b. being sucked into the belly of a flatulent space alien.
   c. being seduced by a many-tentacled alien of indeterminate gender.

5. Do you have a family history of any of the following (Circle where applicable):
   a. schizophrenia
   b. pyromania
   c. paganophobia
   d. kleptomania
   e. necrophilia
   f. xenophobia

6. Do you see a glass as __________
   a. half empty
   b. half full
   c. a window into another dimension

7. If approached by a two-toed sloopery snitch, you would __________
   a. invite him in for coffee.
   b. blow his brains to Kingdom Come.
   c. ask him what happened to his other eight toes.

8. Which of the following factors prompted you to join the MIB?
   a. The chance to fight for truth, justice, and the American way.
   b. A moral obligation to safeguard the citizens of planet Earth.
   c. The generous 401K plan.
   d. Alternate option was death by firing squad.

Are you MIB material?

HOW TO IDENTIFY A SPACE ALIEN

A well-trained MIB agent should be able to recognize a space alien even when one is masquerading as a human. Below is a list of telltale signs that can help you identify aliens in human guise.

CLAWS

When retracted, claws—indigenous to both the cephlapoid and Arquillian species—look very much like human fingernails. Fully extended, these razor-sharp talons slice through human flesh like a knife through butter. The claws will involuntarily protrude from the ends of the fingers when the hands are fully spread.

PERSPIRATION

Baltians, Slabobians, and Martians don't sweat. They pant like dogs. A home without deodorant in the medicine cabinet is indicative of alien activity. It is also possible that the inhabitants are European.

GILLS

Certain aliens—namely cephalopods and Orkans—do not breathe oxygen. They filter air through gills that are hidden behind the eyelids. These gills are visible for a fraction of a second each time the creature blinks.

FEEDING HABITS

Space aliens love Spam. It is considered a delicacy in both the Zeldor and Omega Nine galaxies. Anyone seen eating Spam should be immediately suspected and detained for further questioning.

SKIN

Sinaleans molt their skin twice a year on the eve of the winter and summer solstice. The new skin is smooth as a baby's butt. Later the outer layer becomes crusty and callused—eventually taking on the feel and appearance of sandpaper. At certain times the year, a firm handshake may be all that's necessary to justify an arrest.

ALLERGIES

Aliens, excluding Bugs and Oomish Kanish, are allergic to chocolate. The enzyme necessary for cocoa digestion is missing. As a result, consumption of chocolate bars, cakes, cookies, or other baked goods can produce bloating, gastrointestinal discomfort, and vomiting. It may also cause uncontrollable drooling, convulsions, and a bright red body rash.

ALIEN PENAL CODES

The following laws apply to aliens during their stay on planet Earth. A copy of these laws shall be disseminated to all intergalactic visitors upon arrival.

Alien Ordinance # 371.43.E (Exposure) Aliens are not to disclose their true identity. An alien who reveals or threatens to reveal him/her/itself may have his/her/its visa immediately revoked. Furthermore, the alien can be fined up to two million space rooples.

Alien Ordinance # 900.34.B (Parking) A full-size spacecraft may not be parked in a compact spacecraft parking space. Violators will be ticketed and towed.

Alien Ordinance # 8675.30.M (Trespassing) Aliens found wandering outside their designated zone area shall be considered absent without leave. If found, said alien shall be immediately deported.

AMERICA'S MOST

NAME:
Elby-17

HUMAN ALIAS:
Harold Dweeble

AKA:
Lobster Boy

OFTEN DISGUISED AS:
Computer programmer with sweet tooth

DATE OF BIRTH:
2021 (time traveler)

RACE:
Bipodic crustacean

SEX: **Male**

HEIGHT: **5'11"**

WEIGHT: **160 lbs.**

WEAKNESSES:
Boiling water, melted butter

CRIME:
Massive chocolate theft

SPECIAL NOTE:
Appears harmless, but looks *can* kill

NAME:
Mita Chondria

HUMAN ALIAS:
Bernadette Holdridge

AKA:
Bubbles, Big Mama, Lady Lust

OFTEN DISGUISED AS:
Massage therapist

DATE OF BIRTH:
September 7, 1972

RACE:
Riggilian

SEX: **Female**

HEIGHT: **5' 7" (5' 9" in heels)**

WEIGHT: **120 lbs.**

WEAKNESSES:
Men with dimples

CRIME:
Selling humans for alien experimentation

SPECIAL NOTE:
Highly dangerous. Invites men home; paralyzes them with a kiss

NAME:
Yikem Xexaco

HUMAN ALIAS:
José Gonzales

AKA:
Mikey

OFTEN DISGUISED AS:
Mexican migrant laborer

DATE OF BIRTH:
June 21, 1496

RACE:
Samarium, amphibious bipedal form

SEX: **Male**

HEIGHT: **4'6"**

WEIGHT: **160 lbs.**

WEAKNESSES:
Needs 10,000 calories per day to sustain life

CRIME:
Introduced alien artichoke species with nonremovable spines

SPECIAL NOTE:
Violent and wildly unpredictable

WANTED ALIENS

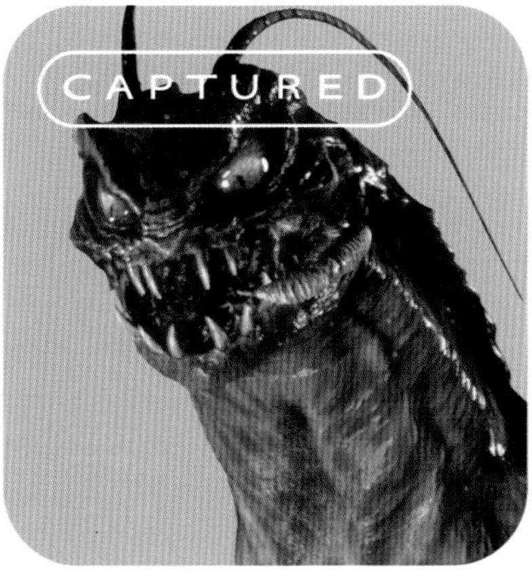

NAME:
EdgarBug

HUMAN ALIAS:
Edgar Smith

AKA:
Lintboy, Boogler, Shmegley

OFTEN DISGUISED AS:
Exterminator

DATE OF BIRTH:
September 5, 1994

SEX: **Male**

HEIGHT: **12' 2"**

WEIGHT: **728 lbs.**

WEAKNESS:
Raid Roach & Ant Killer

CRIME:
Galaxy-napping

SPECIAL NOTE:
This is the most vile creature in the universe

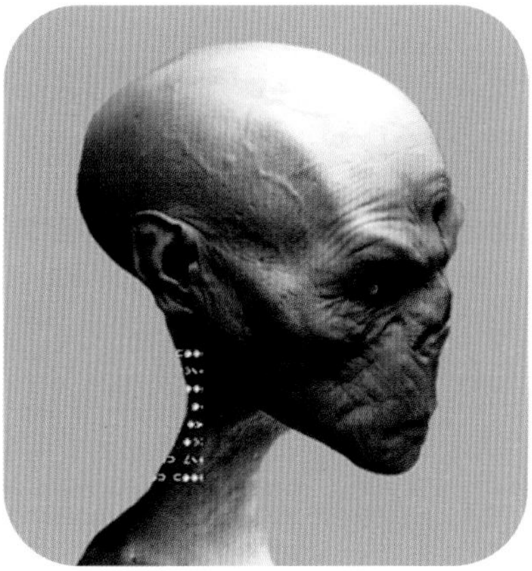

NAME:
Rolling Fish-Goat

HUMAN ALIAS:
Elmore Egghead

AKA:
Skulk, Pesci-Capra

OFTEN DISGUISED AS:
Guidance counselor

DATE OF BIRTH:
January 24, 1812

RACE:
Zeta Reticuli, capacious cranium anthropoid

SEX:
1/2 Male, 1/2 Female

HEIGHT: **3' 9"**

WEIGHT: **146 lbs.**

WEAKNESSES:
Anchovy pizza

CRIME:
Promulgating techno-rock

SPECIAL NOTE:
Prepares for combat by smacking self on head repeatedly

NAME:
Bobo the Squat

HUMAN ALIAS:
Henry Marge Thomas

AKA:
Gator, Mugsy, Vent-head

OFTEN DISGUISED AS:
Disgruntled postal worker

DATE OF BIRTH:
April 9, 600 B.C.

RACE: **Ytterbium**

SEX: **Unknown**

HEIGHT: **3' 2"**

WEIGHT: **250 lbs.**

WEAKNESSES:
Extra-dry skin; needs constant moisturizing

CRIME:
Conspiracy to expose true alien identity

SPECIAL NOTE:
Aggressive and destructive; an intergalactic bad seed

TAKING A SUSPECT INTO CUSTODY

Space aliens, like humans, are entitled to due process. But if proper procedures are not followed, a guilty space alien could walk on a technicality. Therefore it is essential that agents adhere to the following procedures when taking a suspect into custody:

- Read suspect his/her Miranda rights.
- Once suspect has acknowledged that he/she understands these rights, he/she can be handcuffed. (Suspects without hands shall be cuffed around the tentacles.)
- Drive suspect to MiB headquarters for questioning.
- A criminal activity report (see page 79) must be filled out in triplicate and filed with Office of Alien Misconduct.
- Take alien's finger/tentacle prints.
- Take the alien's mug shot. Aliens of multiple form—be it animal, mineral, or vegetable—must be photographed in each of their various guises.
- Allow suspects to make one phone call before placing them in a holding cell. Calls within the 999 galaxy code will be paid for by the MIB. Aliens who wish to call outside the solar system must pay for the call with a credit card or reverse the charges.

SECURING THE CRIME SCENE

An MIB agent's role at the crime scene is twofold. First, make sure that the evidence is collected and recorded in a timely and orderly manner. Second, question any and all witnesses and then immediately erase their memory of the event. (See Permissible Use of a Neuralyzer, page 83.)

Only persons who have legitimate investigative interest should be allowed into a crime scene. Superfluous humans at a crime scene can lead to evidence being moved or destroyed before its value as evidence is recognized. Studies consistently show that too many cooks spoil the stew.

To ensure that important evidence is not overlooked, the following collection procedures should be routinely observed:

1. Photograph the crime scene before it has been disturbed.

2. Decide on a search pattern, i.e. lane, grid, spiral or zone search.

3. Take special note of evidence that can be easily destroyed, such as hoof prints in dust, slime deposits, and molted skin.

4. Cover up any trace of alien activity—e.g., remove dead aliens or body parts.

5. Call for a Containment Unit if backup is needed, or for pick-up of abandoned spacecraft.

Even aliens get towed in Manhattan.

MEN IN BLACK

CRIMINAL ACTIVITY REPORT

Suspect's name MIKEY

Address 911 ELM STREET Planet SAMORIA

Solar System OMEGA 19 Galaxy I/T

Eye color ______ Fur color (if applicable) ______ Antennae Y ☐ N ☑

Height 4'6 Weight 85 Other distinguishing marks TATTOO ON LEFT SHOULDER BLADE, "ALIENS MAKE BETTER LOVERS"

Nature of crime: INTRODUCED ALIEN ARTICHOKE SPECIES WITH NONREMOVABLE SPINES

This is a violation of:

- ☑ State law
- ☑ Universal law
- ☑ Federal law
- ☐ Newton's law
- ☑ Interplanetary law
- ☐ Murphy's law

Location of crime: RURAL AREA NEAR BROWNSVILLE, TEXAS

(If place of business, state name and address of establishment)

Crime occured (on)/between this day/date 5·26·97 and ______

Was a vehicle involved in this crime? Y ☑ N ☐

If Yes, answer the following:

Vehicle type: ☐ UFO ☐ Rocket ☐ Sport Utility Vehicle ☐ Car ☑ Van

Color ______ Year 89 Make ______ Model ______

☑ Stored/impounded

Narrative: In your own words, describe the facts surrounding the arrest:

SUSPECT WAS POSING AS ONE OF A GROUP OF MEXICAN IMMIGRANTS WHEN APPROACHED BY MIB AGENTS. WHEN SUSPECT FAILED TO RESPOND TO QUESTIONS ASKED OF HIM IN SPANISH, AGENT KAY TOOK HIM INTO CUSTODY. SUBJECT ATTEMPTED TO FLEE AND AS A RESULT HE WAS VAPORIZED INTO A GEYSER OF BLUE GOO.

TRANSPO

The MIB has a fleet of 12 specially equipped Ford LTDS for use by agents on street beats. All cars are parked in the agency parking structure. Take the elevators to sub-level five. Keys are to be left in the ignition. You may bring your parking stub to the fourth-floor reception desk for validation.

FAST FORWARD
To defy gravity and travel at speeds in excess of 400 miles per hour, press the red button on the console between the two front seats. New agents should be cautioned against accidental activation of this feature.

FUNNY FUMES
To expel laughing gas from the exhaust pipe, move the gear shift into Drive Three. Any and all aliens within a 30-foot radius of the car will be immobilized by uncontrollable fits of laughter. (Sineleans seem not to be affected, as they have no sense of humor.)

FLOATABLE TIRES
When submerged in more than two feet of water, tires will hyperinflate, making car buoyant.

RTATION

All vehicles are equipped with an AM/FM stereo, air-conditioning, power steering, power windows and locks, as well as a few additional features outlined on the diagram below.

BULLETPROOF WINDSHIELD
The windows of the LTD are impervious to bullets. However, agents are advised to drive slowly on gravel roads as fast-moving pebbles may cause the glass to crack. Built-in squeegees activate automaticaly to remove bugs—earthly or otherwise—from windshield.

MULTIPLE-USE HEADLIGHTS
For urban night driving, leave the headlights on low beam. On lightly traveled roads, switch the headlights to high beam for better illumination. On roads besieged by alien aggressors switch to super-high beam.The 100,000-watt bulbs are designed to temporarily blind your assailant.

WARNING!

Cars should be fueled with certified rocket fuel only.

WEAPONS CATALOG

On-duty MIB agents must be armed and ready for battle. Firearms should be employed if an agent feels his life, or a fellow human's life is in immediate jeopardy.

All agents will be assigned a firearm. (For a description of MIB-approved weaponry, see below). Agents who opt to use the Series 4 De-Atomizer must first report for a mandatory six-week training course. Use by untrained marksmen is strictly prohibited.

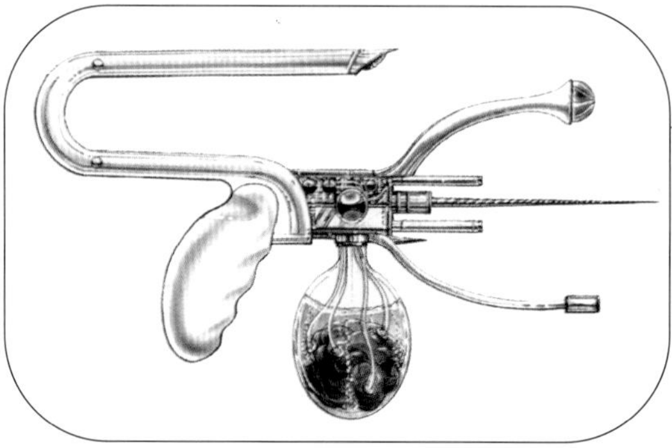

CARBONIZER

A carbonizer with implosion capacity discharges an alien gas called carbon X-11. It has a fogging radius of 100 feet. Fumes are so toxic they can vaporize human flesh in less than 12 seconds. (Available in Midnight Black and Spaceman Silver).

SERIES 4 DE-ATOMIZER

The Series 4 De-Atomizer is a triple-barreled shotgun, with a pump action reloader and a built-in storage clip for 12 additional shells. The rifle can be adjusted to one of the following five settings:

Level 1: Squirt Gun
Level 2: Sling Shot
Level 3: BB Gun
Level 4: Bazooka
Level 5: Atomic machine gun

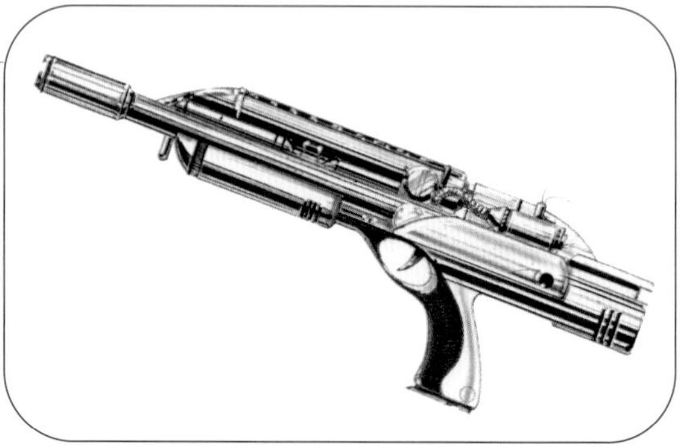

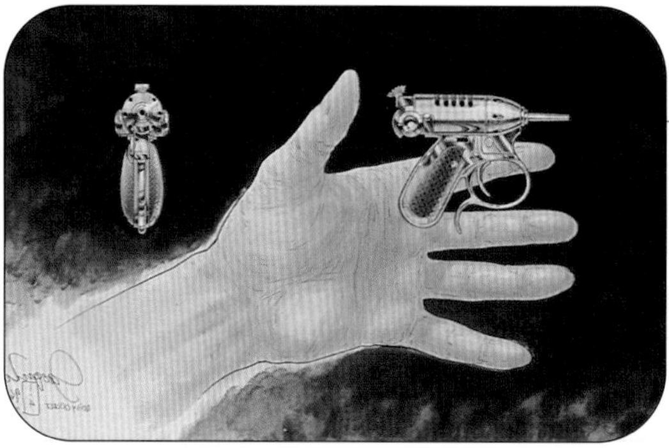

THE NOISY CRICKET

The Noisy Cricket may look harmless, but this lightweight 12-shot handgun is incredibly powerful. The hairpin trigger releases a 110-Grain JHP bullet with 8,932 fps velocity.

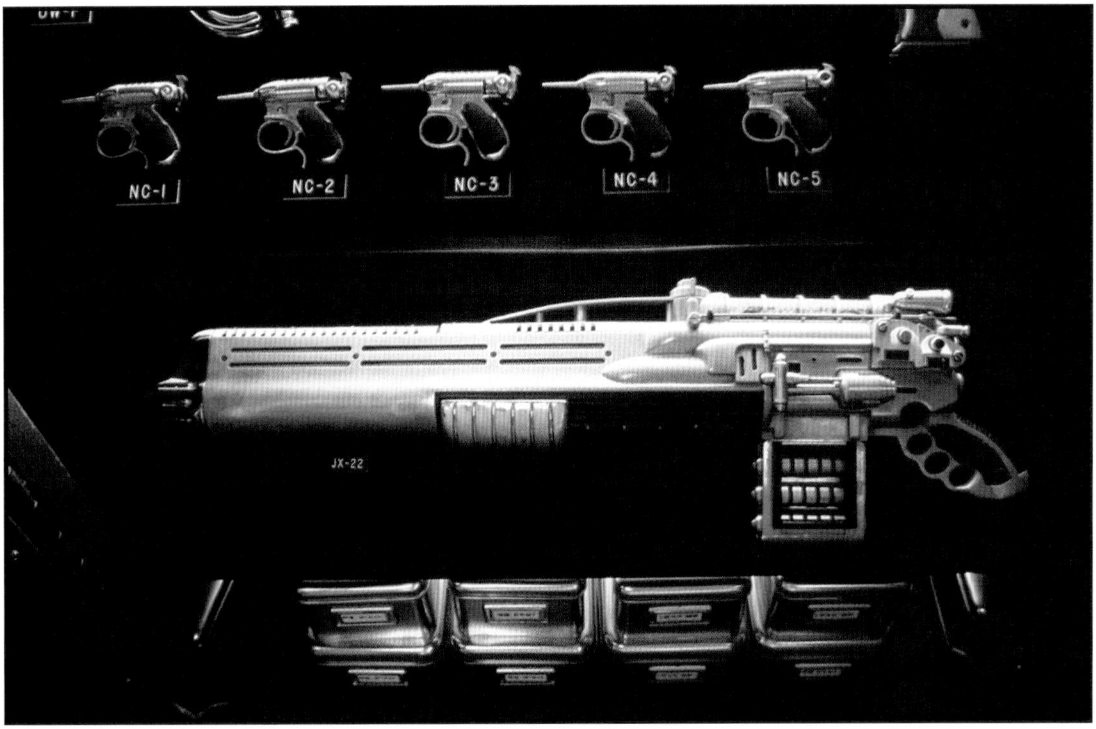

PERMISSIBLE USE OF A NEURALYZER

The neuralyser is an indispensable tool. This instrument emits laser light that can penetrate the human skull and block memory impulses to the brain. If a human accidentally witnesses alien activity, the neuralyzer may be used to erase that memory.

The neuralyzer should not be employed indiscriminately. Agents must decide on a case-by-case basis who and when to neuralyze. If the person witnessing the alien encounter lacks credibility, or if the sighting can somehow be dismissed as a non-alien paranormal phenomenon (ghost, goblin, or poltergeist), refrain from firing. As a general rule, citizens of towns with populations under 150 are not considered credible witnesses.

Agents are required to fill out an incident report form each time they activate the neuralyzer. The report should include time and date of the incident, as well as a detailed description of the lost memory.

Use of a neuralyzer for anything other than official MIB business is a federal offense punishable by up to 50 years in orbit.

Special authorization: Agents who have left behind spouses or significant others are allotted free use of the neuralyzer for conjugal visits. We understand that a wo/man has needs.

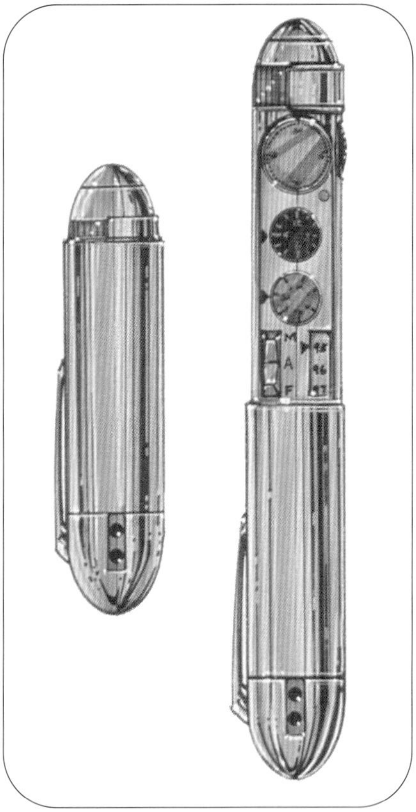

DRESS CODE

MIB agents are impeccably dressed. The uniform should consist of all of the following: black suit, white shirt, black tie, black socks, black shoes, and black sunglasses. We are the Men in Black.

From September through March, suits must be made of worsted wool or wool gabardine. From April until August, cotton or linen. Men in Black do not wear polyester. It's not only ugly, it's highly flammable.

Official underwear style for the MIB is boxers, not briefs. Although briefs supply male genitalia with superior support, they are inherently uncool. Our apologies to former brief wearers for any inconvenience this may cause. Compliance with this dictum is based on the honor system. Skivvies will not be subject to inspection.

Shoe style is the one area where agents are encouraged to express individuality. You may wear black loafers with or without tassels.

Agents receive a clothing allowance of $5,000 a year. This money can be spent only at MIB-approved stores (see your supervisor).

"You'll conform to the identity we give you."

GENERAL APPEARANCE
MIB employees must be adequately dressed for duty. Uniform garments should be properly fitted and maintained in clean, neat and serviceable condition. First impressions are important. Men in Black are Earth's ambassadors and as such are expected to represent the human race in the best possible light.

CLOTHING
Suits should never be worn more than once without being dry-cleaned. Shirts should be laundered using light to medium starch. A company-issue lint brush can be obtained at the MIB's Sanitation Department.

SHAVING
MIB employees are required to shave daily. Agents with particularly sensitive skin must ask their dermatologists to fill out a daily shaving waiver form. Agents who wish to grow a beard or mustache should first seek approval from their supervisor. Sideburns and goatees will not be tolerated. Men in Black set trends. We do not follow them.

UNDERGARMENTS
Wear clean underwear. (In case you get in an accident.)

HAIR
Hair should be kept neat and in a style that's simple and inconspicuous. No restrictions are placed on length, but George Clooney cuts are strongly discouraged. Mohawks, dreadlocks and Jennifer Anistons are strictly prohibited.

THE IMMIGRATION CENTER

IDENTITY CARDS

All aliens are required to register with the Immigration Center upon arrival. First-time visitors must stop by the identity desk to be fitted with a humanoid body and to receive their resident alien cards (See below). Return visitors can proceed immediately to customs. *Special Note: Many aliens request the assumed identity of Elvis Presley. Agents may honor this petition, but restrict subjects' travel to the greater Las Vegas area.*

VISAS

Visas must be obtained at least six weeks prior to arrival. No exceptions. Aliens may apply for a three-week, three-month, or three-year stay. A background check on each applicant must be completed before a visa is issued. If the investigation turns up evidence that the applicant has been convicted of assault, battery, or copyright infringement, access to the planet shall be denied.

TRAVEL RESTRICTIONS

Only visitors with MFA (Most Favored Alien) status can wander the planet freely. The vast majority of aliens shall be restricted to the five boroughs of Manhattan. Requests for alternate destinations will be reviewed on a case-by-case basis. Place a restricted travel stamp on the alien's passport indicating specific latitudinal and longitudinal boundaries. Should an alien need to leave the restricted area, said alien can return to the Immigration Center and apply for a transcontinental day pass.

CUSTOMS

MiB agents have the right to perform a strip search and inspect the body cavities of all suspicious-looking visitors. (Suspect activities include carrying: large quantities of cash, weapons of mass destruction, or vials of virulent bacteria.) Any alien that refuses to be searched shall be immediately deported.

Aliens are forbidden from bringing in foreign fruits or vegetables, unless cleared with agricultural affairs prior to landing. Unauthorized produce will be confiscated and eaten.

HEADQUARTERS PROTOCOLS

ARRIVAL AND DEPARTURE

Concealing the whereabouts of the MIB headquarters is a matter of intergalactic security. Agents are to exercise extreme caution when entering or exiting the building. When departing, keep your head down, and merge with the sidewalk traffic. When returning to headquarters, it is imperative that agents refrain from singing "I'm a Yankee Doodle Dandy" at the top of your lungs, as this tends to attract unnecessary attention.

INTERGALACTIC DATING

If an MIB agent should decide to pursue a relationship with an otherworldly being, the policy is as follows: Don't ask, don't tell, and practice safe sex. The agency neither condones nor condemns intergalactic dating. But be forewarned: Should an MiB agent impregnate or be impregnated by an alien, intergalactic law mandates that sole custody of the offspring be given to the being of higher intelligence. (The only beings less intelligent than humans are space slugs and asteroid mites.)

WORK HOURS

MIB agents work on Centuarian time (a 37-hour day). Of that day, agents are on duty 16 hours. If it is necessary for you to work overtime, you will be paid for additional service at a rate of one and a half times your hourly rate. Vacation days can be taken once in a blue moon.

The following holidays are observed by the MIB:

New Years Day, January 1

Martin Luther King's Birthday, the second Monday in January

Intergalactic Unity Day, February 10

Memorial Day, the last Monday in May

Extraterrestrial Appreciation Day, June 24

Independence Day, July 4

Yom Kippur, the 10th day of Tishri

Christmas, December 25

WARNING!

The contents of this manual are fully protected
under intergalactic copyright law.

Unauthorized Users Will Be Neuralyzed!

CLASSIFIED

MIB
MEN IN BLACK

Protecting the Earth
from the
Scum
of the
Universe
THE SCREENPLAY

1 EXT. ROAD—TEXAS/MEXICO BORDER—NIGHT 1

A million stars wink in the night desert sky. Down here on earth, an insect, one of those big, beautiful, multicolored four-winged jobs, glides effortlessly on the breeze, wafting along through the crisp Texas air.

The insect dips, it banks, it does loop-the-loops—

—and then SPLATS unceremoniously against the windshield of a white van that's tearing down the road.

2 INT. VAN—TEXAS/MEXICO BORDER—NIGHT 2

The DRIVER of the van, a fifty-year-old American, turns on the wipers, smearing the remains all over.

DRIVER

Goddamn bugs.

He squirts some wiper fluid onto the glass, which clears it up a bit, but now he sees something worse up ahead. It's a grouping of headlights, eight of them, all pointed at him, sealing off the road.

He bites his lip and calls over his shoulder, to the back of the van. He speaks in Spanish, which is subtitled.

DRIVER (CONT'D)

Deja me hablar.

(Let me do the talking.)

3 EXT. ROAD—TEXAS/MEXICO BORDER—NIGHT 3

The van slows to a stop in front of the parked cars, all government-issue four doors with "INS" stenciled on the sides. Seven or eight INS AGENTS stand in front of the cars imposingly. Their apparent leader steps forward and comes to the window.

The DRIVER rolls it down. AGENT JANUS, blonde-haired, blue-eyed, also government issue, looks at him and sighs.

AGENT JANUS

Well. Nick the Dick. What a surprise. Where you comin' from?

DRIVER

I was fishing in Cuernavaca.

AGENT JANUS

Sure you were. What do you say we have a look at your catch?

AT THE BACK OF THE VAN,

the Agents fling open the rear doors, revealing a DOZEN FRIGHTENED MEXICANS, hopeful immigrants without official permission. Agent Janus looks at the Driver, who's now held by two other Agents, and shakes his head.

AGENT JANUS

Me, I woulda thrown 'em back.

(to the passengers, in Spanish)

Vamanos. Fuera. Hagan una lina!

(Let's go. Out. Form a line!)

They pile out of the van. Some are parents with small children.

AGENT JANUS (CONT'D)

What do you get, Nick? Hundred bucks a head? Two hundred? I hope you saved it all for your lawyer, pal, 'cause you're gonna need—

He stops in the middle of his sentence, as another car is approaching, fast, its engine WHINING as it barrels down the road toward them. Several Agents pull their weapons.

The new car pulls a hard right, goes off the road, spins around the INS cars, and SQUEALS to a sideways halt, silhouetted in front of their headlights. It's a boxy, black 1986 Ford LTD.

TWO MEN get out, dressed in plain black suits, crisp white shirts, simple black ties, shiny black shoes. KAY, fiftyish, is the apotheosis of world-weary; his partner, DEE, mid-sixties, is just weary. They approach the INS agents.

KAY

We'll take it from here.

AGENT JANUS

Who the hell are you?

Kay and Dee flash some form of ID.

KAY

INS Division 6.

AGENT JANUS

Division 6? I never heard of Division 6.

KAY

Really?

Kay and Dee move past him and approach the row of nervous immigrants.

KAY (CONT'D)

What're we thinking, Dee?

DEE

Tough call, Kay.

He walks down the row, studying the faces, greeting each one cheerily in Spanish.

KAY

!Oye! Que pasa, como estas? Hey!

(What's up, how are you?)

No se preocupe, abuela. Bienvenida a los Estados Unidos.

(Don't worry grandma. Welcome to the United States.)

(next)

A donde vas? San Antonio? Buscando trabajo, no? Buena suerta.

(Where are you going? San Antonio?
Looking for work, aren't you?
Good luck.)

(next)

Es un placer verle aqui.
(It's a pleasure seeing you here.)

One by one, their faces relax, reassured by Kay's calm demeanor. When he reaches the fifth Guy, he keeps the same cheery tone, but:

KAY (CONT'D)

Que dices si te rompo la cara?
(What do you say if I break your face?)

The Guy smiles and nods. Kay stops. His own smile broadens and he drops a hand on the Guy's shoulder.

KAY (CONT'D)

No hablas ni una palabra del Espanol, verdad, amigo?
(You don't speak a word of Spanish, right, friend?)

Again, the Guy smiles and nods. Kay looks back at Dee.

KAY (CONT'D)

We got a winner.

(to the others)

Los restos estan libres a irse. Largense!
(The rest of you are free to go. Scram!)

AGENT JANUS

Sir!

KAY

Tomen el camion, y vayeuse.
(Get on the road and go.)

AGENT JANUS

Sir, you can't just—

KAY

Don't "Sir" me! You have no *idea* who you're dealing with!

Silence on the road. The Driver grins, jumps back in the front seat of the van. The others pile into the rear and they tear out of there.

KAY (CONT'D)

(to Janus)

We're gonna have a little chat with our friend here. You boys can hit the road...and keep on protecting us from dangerous aliens.

Kay and Dee escort their captive across the road and over a small rise, leaving the stunned INS agents standing alone in the roadway.

AGENT JANUS

You ever heard of Division 6?

2ND INS AGENT

There *is* no Division 6.

3RD INS AGENT

Who *are* those guys?

4 EXT. DESERT CLEARING—NIGHT 4

Kay and Dee lead their captive into a clearing in the desert brush. Dee pulls an enormous handgun from a shoulder holster and stays a pace or two off, covering him. Kay has an arm draped around the man's shoulders.

KAY

I think you jumped off the bus in the wrong part of town, amigo. In fact, I'll bet dollars to pesos that you're not—

He pulls out a small laser device, which he ZIPS neatly down the front of the man's clothes.

KAY (CONT'D)

—from anywhere *near* here.

The man's clothes fall to the ground, revealing what he *really* is underneath—A SCALY SPACE BASTARD, about four-and-a-half feet tall, with a snouth, snail-like tentacles, and independently moving eyes on stalks at the top of his head.

The only part of his camouflage not crumpled to the ground is the humanesque "head," which he still lamely holds in one of his hands. It's propped up by a stick, like a puppet, and it continues to make expressions as he holds it.

KAY (CONT'D)

Mikey?! When did they let *you* out of jail?

MIKEY replies—an unfathomable combination of GRUNTS, SQUEAKS, and saliva.

KAY (CONT'D)

Political refugee. Right.

DEE

You know how many treaty articles you've just violated?

Mikey makes a lame SQUEAK.

KAY

One, my ass. Try seven.

DEE

From unauthorized immigration to failure to properly inoculate prior to landing.

KAY

(off Mikey's objections)

Okay, that's enough. Hand me your head and put up your arms.

From behind Mikey, they hear a terrified GASP.

Kay and Dee both look over quickly. One of the alien's eyes, on a tall stalk, whips around too. All three of them see AGENT JANUS, standing just over the rise, staring in frozen amazement.

KAY (CONT'D)

Ah, shit.

Agent Janus SCREAMS. Mikey rips free of the rest of the "Mexican" disguise, knocks Dee out of the way, and takes off straight at Janus, SCREECHING a horrible Space Bastard screech. Janus freezes, terrified.

KAY (CONT'D)

Dee! Shoot him!

Dee struggles to roll over and change the controls on his gun, which fell out of his hand as he hit the ground.

KAY (CONT'D)

Dee, for Christ's—

Mikey keeps moving, covering the last few yards to Janus quickly. He steps on a rock, launches himself into the air, his dripping jaws cranked wide open—

—there is a SIZZLING sound, a brilliant white flash—

—and Mikey ERUPTS in a geyser of blue goo that splatters all over the ground, the trees, and Agent Janus' face. Behind where Mikey was, Kay stands, smoking weapon in hand.

5 EXT. ROAD—TESAS/MEXICO BORDER—NIGHT 5

On the road, the INS AGENTS pull their guns and run toward the rise.

6 EXT. DESERT CLEARING—NIGHT 6

Kay has an arm around Janus, whom he is leading further into the clearing. Janus is white, shaking, eyes like silver dollars.

AGENT JANUS

Th— th— th—

KAY

(helping)

"That."

AGENT JANUS

That wasn't— wasn't— wasn't—

KAY

Human, I know. Oops. Got some entrails on you.

He takes out a handkerchief and wipes off the Agent's face. As he does, Janus looks back to where Mikey blew up. Then at Kay. And then up at the stars.

The other INS Agents burst over the rise, SHOUTING questions.

KAY

Okay, everybody, situation's under control, calm down. If you'll just give me your attention for a moment I'll tell you what happened.

From over the rise, car engines WHINE in the distance and headlights start to flash around them. Kay reaches into his pocket and pulls out a tubular metallic device the size of a pocket recorder. He checks his watch, figures in his head, then dials an electronic counter on the side of the device up to "08."

KAY (CONT'D)

This is called a "neuralyzer." A gift from some friends from out of town. The red eye here isolates and measures the electronic impulses in your brain. More specifically, the ones for memory.

Behind him, six more MEN IN BLACK, all wearing black suits and sunglasses, come over the hill. Kay barks a few orders to them.

KAY (CONT'D)

Gimme a splay burn on the perimeter, please; holes at 40, 60, and 80.

2ND INS AGENT

What in the hell is going on?!

KAY

Exactly the right question. And the answer lies right—here. Pay attention.

JANUS

Who are you, really?

KAY

Really? I'm just a figment of your imagination.

He holds up the neuralyzer. The Agents peer closely at it. Kay reaches into his pocket, puts on his own black sunglasses—

—and pushes a button on the side of the neuralyzer. A BLINDING FLASH a tenth of a second long sears the Agents' eyeballs. They stare blankly.

KAY (CONT'D)

God, we're a gullible breed.

Behind him, TONGUES OF FIRE blast from a flame thrower held by one of the Men in Black. Kay looks back at the INS Agents, who are just coming around, as if awakening from a concussion.

KAY (CONT'D)

I mean it, fellas, you are lucky to be alive after a blast like that.

The Agents look around, confused.

AGENT JANUS

What—blast?

Kay gestures behind him, where the Men in Black are now using fire extinguishers to douse the flames they themselves started.

KAY

Underground gas vein, genius. You guys need to exercise more caution before discharging your firearms.

He jabs a finger into Janus' chest.

KAY (CONT'D)

Especially *you*.

Dee has moved away from them all and is sitting on a rock, staring up at the night sky, his sunglasses dangling idly from one hand. Kay steps away from the group and finds him. He sits down next to him.

DEE

I'm sorry. About...back there.

KAY

Happens.

DEE

Didn't used to.

He holds up his hands, which tremble with age.

DEE (CONT'D)

The spirit's willing, Kay, but the rest of me...

He looks up, at the million stars shining overhead.

DEE (CONT'D)

They're beautiful, aren't they?

KAY

What?

DEE

The stars. We never just—*look*. Anymore.
(back to Kay)
I'll tell ya, Kay. I will miss the chase.

Kay pulls his neuralyzer from his pocket and looks down at it.

KAY

No. You won't.

A8 EXT. GRAND CENTRAL STATION—SOUTHERN EXPOSURE—NIGHT A8

A shot of the clock on the Station's stately southern exposure. WE PAN DOWN TO...

A pair of feet running. They belong to a man we will know as the PERPETRATOR. As we track with him, he SPEEDS UP and OUT OF FRAME.

A new set of feet come into frame. These belong to JAMES EDWARDS, a NYC COP in undercover street clothes. In the BACKGROUND, about ten feet behind, are two other cops, trying to keep up.

Edwards is a lot faster, though. He pulls out his badge that hangs from a chain under his shirt.

EDWARDS

Stop! NYPD!

He continues running, out of frame, and we stay on one of the other COPS, overweight, who gives up the chase and drops to his knees, heaving air.

COP

All yours, Edwards!

The Cop fumbles in his pocket for a pack of cigarettes.

TRACK WITH EDWARDS AND THE PERP

As they run down the bridge that traverses Park Avenue in the low Forties. The Perp veers to the left and, seemingly oblivious to the fact that it's a thirty- foot drop, he hurdles the guard rail, and drops to Forty-first Street below.

EDWARDS is surprised by this maneuver, but doesn't waste a second. He, too, hurdles the guard rail and lands on...

B8 EXT. 41ST STREET AND PARK AVENUE—NIGHT B8

A DOUBLE-DECKER BUS, one of those cheesy sightseers that hold up midtown traffic. The bus, of course, is completely filled with JAPANESE TOURISTS, and it seems like every single one of them has a video camera.

EDWARDS pushes through the crowd...

EDWARDS

Grand Central Station off to your left, folks...

With the bus still moving, he scrambles down the circular stairs and runs out through the side door.

He spots the Perp, sailing east on Forty-first Street.

EDWARDS

Dammit, man, you're making me sweat up my gear!

Edwards spots one of those *New York Post* delivery trucks, the kind with the open back door, rumbling by. He runs and jumps into the back.

C8 EXT. FIFTH AVENUE—NIGHT C8

THE PERP, meanwhile, is running at top speed, when Edwards glides into frame, leaning off the back of the truck.

EDWARDS

Yo, man, your luck just ran out.

He leaps from the back of the moving truck and tackles the Perp.

The Perp, now straddled by Edwards, is terrified.

PERP

He's coming! He's coming!

EDWARDS

And when he gets here, I'll kick his ass too.

Edwards is about to slap the cuffs on him, when the Perp blinks. Nothing unusual about that, but then another set of translucent, milky white eyelids, underneath his regular eyelids, blinks also.

Edwards is thrown for a moment, which is all the time the Perp needs to pull out...

His WEAPON, which is the strangest looking gun you've ever seen. Reacting quickly, Edwards bats it out of the Perp's hand.

THE WEAPON smashes into the stone wall surrounding Central Park and SHATTERS into a million pieces.

EDWARDS

What the...

WHOMP! The Perp kicks him in the nuts, then scrambles to his feet and takes off again. Edwards staggers after him, in pain.

The Perp leaps over a moving car, towards the GUGGENHEIM MUSEUM. Edwards tries to follow, but a bus pulls in front of him. After it passes, the Perp is gone.

9 EXT. GUGGENHEIM MUSEUM—NIGHT 9

Edwards runs over to the Museum, leans over the wall that surrounds it, and in the next instant...

The Perp flies past him, having leapt from twenty feet down to the top of the Guggenheim. He scrambles up and over the ledge.

Edward reacts. He runs to the front door of the Museum, shoots it open and runs inside.

He runs from the rotunda up the grand ramp of the Guggenheim.

10 EXT. GUGGENHEIM MUSEUM—ROOF—NIGHT 10

On the roof, the PERP reaches the top, climbs over the edge, and CRUNCHES to the gravel surface. He leaps to his feet and races over to a door. It's locked.

He tugs on another. It's locked too. He pulls on a third. It swings open—

—*revealing EDWARDS on the other side*, breathing hard. He aims his weapon at the Perp.

EDWARDS

Wassup?

The Perp SCREAMS inhumanly and panics. He backpedals, toward the edge of the roof.

PERP

He's coming! He's coming because *I failed*, and

now he'll *kill me too!*

EDWARDS

Stop!

PERP

You don't understand. Your world is gonna end.

But the Perp has backed right into the edge of the roof, and now he starts to fall over. The Perp blinks.

EDWARDS

What are you?!

The Perp looks down. He decides.

—and he falls, SCREAMING, to his death.

CUT TO:

11 INT. INTERROGATION ROOM—NIGHT 11

EDWARDS sits on one side of the table, a POLICE INSPECTOR and a UNIFORMED SERGEANT (the one who gave up the chase and lit a cigarette earlier), sit across from him.

INSPECTOR

Perpetrator then blinked two sets of eyelids. You mean blinked with both eyes?

EDWARDS

No, sir. He blinked once with one set, then again with another completely different set.

SERGEANT

Sort of a low beam, high beam.

INSPECTOR

Was that before or after he drew the weapon which you claim evaporated into a million pieces?

EDWARDS

After, sir.

INSPECTOR

And why do you suppose none of the other officers saw either of these two events?

EDWARDS

'Cause some of the other officers are a little soggy in the midsection. And they couldn't keep up, sir.

SERGEANT

Hey, Edwards, if you were half the man I am—

EDWARDS

What do you mean? I *am* half the man you are.

SERGEANT

What the hell is your problem?

EDWARDS

My problem is you being all up in my damn face all the time.

SERGEANT

I think he threw him off the roof. Ten minutes—your best shot.

INSPECTOR

(cutting off the Sergeant)

Sergeant. I want to talk to you outside. Now.

EDWARDS

You need ten minutes on a Stairmaster, you pudgy bastard.

12 INT. INTERROGATION ROOM—LATER—NIGHT 12

A woman sneaks into the room. DOCTOR LAUREL WEAVER, thirtyish, dark-haired, dark-eyed, general aura of darkness around her, stands above him. Laurel looks like she was just dragged out of bed (which she was) and saw a spaceman (which she did).

She looks over her shoulder once, then whispers to him.

LAUREL

Laurel Weaver. Deputy Medical Examiner. I believe you. I opened him up. Find me at the morgue. On 26th. I'll tell you what I found.

EDWARDS

Hey...Wait a minute. Wait a minute.

LAUREL

(turning at the door)

You have really pretty eyes.

She hurries to turn the corner, but is STOPPED by someone who remains just offscreen.

VOICE (O.S.)

Dr. Weaver, from the coroner's office? Working

on the John Doe?

Edwards twists in his chair, to get a better look. All he sees is Laurel, facing whoever it is in the hallway.

LAUREL

Yes. That's right.

VOICE (O.S.)

Would you look right here, please.

The Someone says something else and Laurel steps forward, now also out of Edwards's line of vision.

LAUREL (O.S.)

Look where?

Edwards stretches even further in his seat, when there is a blinding FLASH from the corridor. *Really* curious now, he starts to get up—

— when KAY steps into the room and closes the door behind him. Edwards rolls his eyes.

KAY

Some night, huh?

EDWARDS

Oh, yeah, some night.

He crosses to the door.

KAY

They were gills.

Edwards stops.

KAY

Not eyelids.

EDWARDS

Who are you?

KAY

Did he say anything to you?

EDWARDS
(scoffing)

Yeah, sure. He said the world was coming to an end.

KAY

Did he say when?

EDWARDS

You're kidding, right?

KAY

Would you recognize his weapon if you saw it again?

EDWARDS

Absolutely.

KAY

Let's take a ride.

EDWARDS

Wait a minute. I got a ton of paperwork.

KAY

It's all done.

At that point, the INSPECTOR sticks his head in, smiles and gives Edwards the thumbs up.

INSPECTOR

Good work, Edwards.

Edwards looks at the Inspector, then at Kay. As they leave.

KAY

You ran that guy down on foot? That's tough. That's double tough.

CUT TO:

AA12 INT. FORD LTD—A MOMENT LATER—DRIVING AA12

In a plain, boxy Ford, Kay drives, silent. He raises his hand and nods to a black MIB truck coming in the opposite direction.Edwards, in the passenger seat, is still in his undercover outfit.

EDWARDS

So who you with?

Kay says nothing.

EDWARDS (CONT'D)

You got the plain clothes, the government-issued wheels. Secret Service? CIA?

Kay remains utterly silent.

EDWARDS (CONT'D)

(referring to the car)
Yeah, well, whoever it is, you're short on funding.

KAY
Nothing is what it seems, kid.

EDWARDS
Oh, yeah, my bad '86 Ford LTD. *That's* a luxury ride. C'mon, who ya with?

Kay pulls the car to a stop.

KAY
I'm part of a secret organization that monitors and polices alien activity on earth.

Kay opens the door and gets out of the car. Edwards follows.

A12 EXT. PAWN SHOP—NIGHT A12

Edwards looks around. Sees they're standing in front of a PAWN SHOP.

EDWARDS
This is where we're going?

They get out of the car.

EDWARDS (CONT'D)
Jack Jeebs? Guy buys from chain snatchers. Doesn't even *sell* guns.

KAY
Really?

EDWARDS
All right, you think it's worth shaking him up, fine. I'll do my thing. Then I want some answers.

KAY
Do your "thing," kid.

Edwards goes inside.

B12 INT. PAWN SHOP—NIGHT B12

JACK JEEBS is the sleazy, sarcastic proprietor of the Pawn Shop. He's not easily intimidated.

JEEBS
Officer Edwards. Oh, hey, geez, how'd these get here? I thought I turned 'em in to the proper authorities.

He casually brushes some Rolexes off the counter.

EDWARDS
Way I hear it, Jeebs, you into something a little hotter than some stolen Rolexes.

JEEBS
Sure—I'm a big crack dealer now. I just work here because I love the hours.

This pisses Edwards off. He grabs Jeebs by the collar.

EDWARDS
(getting angry)
I'm *talking* about guns, Jeebs. High-tech stuff.

JEEBS
C'mon, Edwards, whatcha see is what I got.

KAY (O.S.)
Why don't you show him the imports, Jeebs.

At the sound of Kay's voice, Jeebs suddenly pales, a look of fear coming over his face.

JEEBS
H-hiya Kay, how are you?

KAY
The imports, Jeebs. Now.

JEEBS
You know I got outta that business a long time ago, Kay.

KAY
Why do you lie to me? I hate it when you lie.

He pulls his own gun and aims it at Jeebs' forehead.

JEEBS
Whoa, whoa, Kay, hold on a minute here...

KAY
I'm going to count to three.

Edwards, seeing that Kay is getting somewhere, joins in the routine.

EDWARDS
He'll do it, Jeebs.

KAY
One.

EDWARDS
I've *seen* him do it.

KAY
Two.

EDWARDS
Talk to *me*, Jeebs, he's crazy when he's like this.

JEEBS
He's *always* crazy.
(to Kay)
Take a cruise. Get a massage—

KAY

Three.

KA-BOOM! Kay blows Jeebs' head off and Jeebs' body collapses to the floor. Edwards is shocked.

Edwards pulls his own weapon and points it at Kay's head.

EDWARDS

Put down the gun and put your hands on the counter!

KAY

I warned him.

EDWARDS

Drop the weapon!

KAY

You warned him.

EDWARDS

You are under arrest. You have the right to remain silent.

KAY

Will you relax?

JEEBS (O.S.)
(irritated)

Don't *do* that.

Edwards whirls around to see Jeebs' BODY, growing another head. Only takes four or five seconds. Kay calmly shoves his gun up against Jeebs' baby-soft new cheek.

JEEBS (CONT'D)

Do you know how much that hurts?

KAY

Show us what you got, Jeebs. Or I'll use up another one.

Jeebs, panicked, hits a button on the underside of the counter, which promptly flips over, revealing yet another dusty shelf, piled high with junk—

—but this is all alien junk. Weapons, mostly, bizarre, otherworldly weapons of all shapes and sizes.

KAY

Edwards?

Edwards, still dazed by Jeebs' regrown head, glances down at all the weapons.

EDWARDS

Uh, this. This is what I saw.

Kay looks at Jeebs, pissed off.

KAY

You sold a carbonizer with implosion capacity to an unlicensed cephlapoid.

JEEBS

He looked all right to me.

KAY

A carbonizer is an assassin's weapon, Jeebs. Who was the target?

JEEBS

I don't know.

Kay raises the weapon again, threatening.

KAY

Jeebs!

JEEBS

I don't know!

Kay lowers his gun, gestures to the shelf full of weapons.

KAY

This is all confiscated. All of it. I want you on the next transport off this rock. Or I'll shoot you where it doesn't grow back.

Jeebs nods, point taken. Kay leaves.

EDWARDS

Yeah. I'll be by tomorrow for those Rolexes.

Shaken, Edwards follows.

C12 EXT. PAWN SHOP—NIGHT C12

Edwards staggers out of the shop, trying to get the day's events straight in his head.

EDWARDS

The eyelids, fine...and the jumping thing...and the gun...okay, but the head?

KAY

Searching for a handle on the moment here? A place to file all this.

EDWARDS

See a head doesn't do that, it doesn't just grow back.

(looking up)

What's going on?

KAY

Can't help you, kid. Only comfort I can offer is that tomorrow, you won't remember a thing.

EDWARDS

Oh, no. *This* I'm gonna remember for a long, long time.

Kay pulls the neuralyzer from his pocket. He hesitates for the briefest of moments—as if this particular neuralyzation is different than all the others.

Then he puts on his sunglasses.

KAY

Ever see one of these?

CUT TO:

13 INT. CHINESE RESTAURANT—NIGHT 13

—the flash dims on EDWARDS and KAY, sitting at a table in a Chinese restaurant.

KAY

(finishing a joke)

—and the wife says yeah, Harry, I know, but this one's eating my popcorn!

He busts out laughing. Edwards, across from him, is completely disoriented. He looks down. There's a half- eaten order of broccoli beef and several empty bottles of beer on the table in front of him.

EDWARDS

Huh?

Kay checks his watch.

KAY

Whoops. Gotta run. Thanks for the egg rolls.

EDWARDS

Where am I?

KAY

See what I mean about tequila? You're a bright young man, James. Just lay off the sauce. I'll see you tomorrow, nine a.m. sharp.

He turns and walks out. Edwards checks his watch. A WAITRESS appears.

WAITRESS

Another beer?

EDWARDS

Coffee. *Please.*

She walks off. Edwards looks at the table. There is a business card lying next to his plate, on which Kay has handwritten "James D. Edwards, Saturday, 9 a.m., 504 Battery Drive."

Edwards looks at it, puzzled. He turns the card over and looks at the other side. There's not much there, no name, no phone or fax number, no e-mail address. Just three little letters, dead in the middle of the card:

MIB

CUT TO:

14 EXT. FARMHOUSE—NIGHT 14

A lonely farmhouse stands amid the fields of upstate New York farm country. Several lights are on and through a window we can see the silhouette of a MAN sitting at the kitchen table, the silhouette of a WOMAN hovering over him, bringing things to him.

The Man (EDGAR) waves his arms, ranting.

EDGAR (O.S.)

I go out, *I* work my butt off to make a living, all I want is to come home to a nice clean house with a nice fat steak on the table, but instead I get this—this—I don't even know what you *call* this!

In the sky above, it's one of those brilliant star fields. But something strange is happening with one of those stars—it's getting bigger.

EDGAR (O.S.)

I'll tell you what it *looks* like, it *looks* like poison. Don't you take that away, I'm eating that, damn it! It *is* poison, isn't it?!

No, that star isn't getting bigger, it's *moving*. Toward us. Fast. It goes from a pinpoint to a dime, to a nickel, to a quarter, and works its way into fruit metaphors.

EDGAR (O.S.)

I swear to God, I would not be surprised if it was, the way you skulk around here like a dog been hit too much—or ain't been hit enough, I can't make up my mind.

Okay, we're *way* past watermelon now, that thing is *huge*, and it's starting to glow hot red as it enters the earth's atmosphere, headed straight toward us, coming *here*, to Beatrice and Edgar's place.

The blazing fireball barrels through the sky, SNAPS off a couple trees—

EDGAR (O.S.)

You're *useless*, Beatrice! The only thing that pulls its weight around here is my goddamn *truck!*

—and SLAMS right through a pickup truck parked in the driveway. A concussive BLAST follows, then a geyser of smoke and flame erupts.

EDGAR (O.S.)

Stay here!

The silhouette of Edgar leaps to its feet, races to the door, and throws it open. Edgar is everything his voice led us to expect—a nasty, bug-eyed redneck carrying a twelve-gauge shotgun. His mouth agape, he walks across the yard and stares at the hulking shell that was his truck. The skeleton of the truck is still there, but there's a huge,

smoldering hole in it, a hole that goes at least ten feet down into the ground.

EDGAR

Figures.

He walks to the truck and touches the door handle. Hot. Using his shirt tail, he opens the door and peers down into the hole.

IN THE HOLE, he sees a smooth curve of metal and a few blinking lights. Embedded into the ground is, indeed, a spaceship, maybe eight feet across.

BEATRICE calls from behind him, standing in the doorway fearfully.

BEATRICE

What is it, Edgar?!

EDGAR

(turns to her)

Get your big butt back in that house!

Beatrice does as she's told, closing the door behind her. Edgar turns back to the smoldering rock, raising his shotgun in defense. AN OTHERWORLDLY VOICE comes from deep in the hole.

VOICE (O.S.)

Place projectile weapon on ground.

Edgar staggers back a step, terrified. But then he regains himself, raises the weapon, and steps forward, pointing it menacingly down into the hole.

EDGAR

You can have my gun when you pry it from my cold, dead fingers!

There is a pause while the voice thinks about this offer. Finally, it responds, in a voice and cadence remarkably similar to Edgar's.

VOICE (O.S.)

Your proposal is acceptable.

A long, hairy pincer flashes out of the hole, grabs Edgar by the head, and pulls him down into the hole.

From deep in the hole, we hear a terrible RIPPING sound, like a bedsheet being torn in half. There are some disgusting GUSHY sounds, then a moment later, something flies out of the hole and FLOPS onto the ground next to the truck.

It's Edgar. Well, sort of. His body parts still hang together—face, arms, legs, even clothes—but everything inside has been removed and now he just lies there, flat and empty, like a tuxedo on the floor after the prom.

The shotgun flies out and lands beside him.

CUT TO:

15 INT. FARMHOUSE—KITCHEN—NIGHT 15

BEATRICE sits at the kitchen table, terrified, still wiping away tears from Edgar's diatribe. The door opens and EDGAR comes back into the kitchen, seemingly fleshed out again, leaving the door hanging open behind him. He carries the shotgun.

She looks up at him, anxious. But his face is a blank.

BEATRICE

What on earth was it?!

He looks at her strangely. When he speaks, his voice is different than before. More refined.

EDGAR

Sugar.

Pause. She looks out the window, at the smoking truck.

BEATRICE

I've never seen sugar do *that*.

EDGAR

Give me sugar.

Puzzled, Beatrice gets up, goes to the cabinet, and grabs a bag of sugar. She holds it out to him.

EDGAR (CONT'D)

In water.

Frightened, she takes a glass of water from the table. She dumps some of the sugar into it.

EDGAR (CONT'D)

More.

She puts more, till the glass is brimming. She stirs it quickly with a knife and hands it to him, her hand trembling.

Edgar takes it and downs it in a single gulp. Beatrice stares at Edgar, no idea what to think. She notices something odd about the skin on his neck.

BEATRICE

Edgar, your *skin!* It's—it's—just *hanging* off your bones!

Edgar drops the glass and looks in a window, to catch his reflection. He reaches up —

—and *twists* his whole face, as if adjusting a ski mask, then tucks the skin of his neck back into his shirt collar. He looks at her.

EDGAR

That better?

Beatrice faints.

16 EXT. FARMHOUSE—NIGHT 16

Stillness. Silence. A loud SCRAPING sound comes from the pit left by the spaceship.

The nose of the ship itself rises up out of the pit, wavers, keeps moving, and finally CRUNCHES to the ground outside the pit.

EDGAR climbs out of the pit, breathing heavily. He dusts himself off and continues pushing the ship, along the ground, off into the darkness.

CUT TO:

17 EXT. MIB BUILDING—DAY 17

The next morning. EDWARDS, holding the small MIB business card in his hand, compares the address written down by Kay to the address on the utterly nondescript building in front of him. It's seven stories high, gray, windowless, perfectly square, squatting on a bridge over a road like a fat guy on the john.

"504 Battery Drive."

18 INT. MIB BUILDING—TUNNEL VENT ROOM—DAY 18

EDWARDS steps through a heavily barred metal door and into long, bizarre room. One wall is entirely dominated by the enormous blades of a tunnel vent air intake. There is an elevator at the far end of the room and an OLD SECURITY GUARD, the rent-a-cop kind, reading a comic book on a folding metal chair halfway across.

Edwards walks across the room, his footsteps ECHOING. The Guard looks up.

GUARD

Help you?

EDWARDS

Maybe, I'm not sure, see, I got this card—

GUARD

Elevator. Push the "call" button.

And he goes back to his comic book. Edwards, maybe out of nothing more than curiosity at this point, walks across the room, toward the elevator. As he draws close, the elevator doors WHOOSH open, expecting him.

19 INT. MIB BUILDING—ENTRANCE ELEVATOR—DAY 19

Edwards steps inside and turns around. The doors close. He pushes the "call" button and waits, but the elevator doesn't move. Instead, doors on the other side of the elevator slide open silently behind him. Edwards waits, unaware.

From behind him, somebody clears their throat. Edwards turns around, and finds himself standing in—

20 INT. MIB BUILDING—INTERVIEW ROOM—DAY 20

This back room is every bit as mysterious and unfamiliar as the entryway. Standing at the front of the room is ZED, a wire-haired career G-man, an old school bureaucrat, wearing the exact same kind of suit Kay had on last night. SIX OTHER HOT RECRUITS sit in egg-shaped chairs, staring at Edwards.

One chair is empty.

ZED

You're late. Sit down.

Edwards takes the remaining chair. The elevator doors slide shut. Zed continues addressing the Recruits.

ZED (CONT'D)

My name is Zed. You're all here because you're the best of the best. Marines, Navy SEALS, Army Rangers...NYPD.

They all turn and regard Edwards a little smugly. He gives it back.

ZED (CONT'D)

And we're looking for one of you. Just one. What will follow is a series of simple tests designed to quantify motor skills, hand-eye coordination, concentration, stamina—I see we have a question.

Edwards's hand is, indeed, up.

EDWARDS

Why, uh—I'm sorry, it's just no one really asked this, but—why, exactly, are we doing this?

Silence. Then one of the young recruits eagerly raises his hand. Zed calls on him.

ZED

Son?

AMBITIOUS RECRUIT
(loud and formal)

Jake Jensen, West Point, graduate with honors. We're here because you're looking for the best of the best of the best, *sir!*

Edwards tries to stifle a laugh, but can't.

ZED

What's so funny, Edwards?

EDWARDS

I— I don't know, sir. This guy. "Best of the best of the best of the best of the—"

(realizing *nobody* is with him on this)

It just struck me as—

(totally serious)

Humorous. Sir.

Short pause. Then Zed continues.

ZED

Okay. Let's get going.

21 INT. MIB BUILDING—INTERVIEW ROOM—LATER—DAY 21

The recruits scribble away at the written test. It's a thick document—reasoning skills, general knowledge, diagrams. The RECRUITS seem to be really powering through it, filling in answer after answer.

But no desks have been provided for them, and they're all still in their chairs, writing uncomfortably on their thighs or knees.

EDWARDS is really struggling. He writes two words on one answer, then decides to erase it. The lack of a writing surface is driving him crazy; his pencil even TEARS through the page.

He looks up. In the middle of the tile floor, there is an unused table. Edwards gets up, goes to it, grabs hold—

—and drags it, SCREECHING DEAFENINGLY, back to his chair. Everybody looks up, wincing at the horrible sound that fills the room.

Edwards sits back down, now writing on the table. That's better.

Zed raises an eyebrow. He stares at Edwards, then looks up, toward a smoked glass window. Behind the dark glass, a FIGURE stands, staring, unemotional.

CUT TO:

22 INT. MIB BUILDING—SHOOTING GALLERY—DAY 22

SEVEN WEAPONS rest on a table in the middle of an otherwise empty, triangular room. The SEVEN RECRUITS stand in front of the table.

There's an odd moment—where everyone sort of looks around: at each other, at the blank walls...

EDWARDS

Anyone, uh...any of you guys know what we're doing here?

MARINE

(clipped, unquestioning)

Looking for the best of the best of the best.

EDWARDS

(can't help but smile)

Well, yeah, I know, but...

And then . . suddenly—

The two far walls *pull apart*. The whole room pulsates and the air is suddenly filled with a bewildering swirl of stroboscopic images, both human and alien. Everywhere is color, light and movement—a holographic mass of strange shapes and characters moving simultaneously.

The Recruits lunge for the weapons, snapping them up and taking aim. SIX SHOTS are fired at once. And then, a second later, a SEVENTH SHOT is fired. Everyone sort of looks at Edwards, who puts his gun down last.

There's an awkward silence. Then the door opens. Light pours in, and ZED with it. Even the highly competitive cadets can't help but feel some sympathy as Zed walks straight to Edwards.

ZED

The hell happened?

EDWARDS

Hesitated, sir.

Zed looks into the gallery. Most obvious in the frozen tableau of creatures is a lunging, snarling beast, which has three bullet holes in its chest. Next to it is a massively deformed humanoid creature with a large hook for a head, which also has three holes in it. In the back corner of the gallery, there is a single bullet hole in a pretty eight-year-old girl.

ZED

May I ask why you felt little Tiffany deserved to die?

EDWARDS

She was the only one who actually seemed dangerous. At the time.

ZED

And how did you come to that conclusion?

EDWARDS

Hook-head guy. You explain to me how he can think with a hook for a head. Answer; it's not his head. His head is that butt-ugly bean-bag thing over there. 'Cause if you look at the snarling beast-guy, he's not snarling, he's sneezing—he's got tissues in his hand. No threat there, and anyhow, the girl's books were way too advanced for an eight-year-old's. And besides, from where I'm looking, she was the only one who appeared to have a motive. And I don't appreciate your jumping down my throat about it.

Sideways glances from the other recruits. Zed sighs.

EDWARDS (CONT'D)
Or, uh—do I owe her an apology?

CUT TO:

23 INT. MIB BUILDING—OBSERVATION ROOM/ INTERVIEW ROOM—DAY 23

ZED and KAY stand behind smoked glass, staring at the RECRUITS, who are still in the shooting gallery, waiting for a decision.

ZED
He's got a real problem with authority.

KAY
So do I. The guy ran down a cephlapoid, Zed. On *foot*. Tenacity. That I can use.

ZED
I hope you know what you're doing.

Zed turns and walks away. Kay stares through the glass, at EDWARDS, who stands alone on one side of the room, apart from the rest of the group.

Zed reappears on the other side of the glass, coming through a door and into the shooting gallery. As he talks, Kay turns and walks off.

ZED (CONT'D)
Congratulations, you're everything we've come to expect from years of government training. Now, if you'll just follow me, we have one more test to administer, an eye exam.

24 INT. MIB BUILDING—HALLWAY—DAY 24

The RECRUITS follow ZED out of the shooting gallery and into a long hallway. Zed motions them off to the left. EDWARDS is the last one out of the room, but he stops as he steps into the hallway.

KAY is outside the door, waiting for him. Edwards recognizes him from last night.

EDWARDS
You! Hey, what's goin' on?

The other recruits continue down the hall with Zed. Kay doesn't answer, just gestures to Edwards to follow him down the hall, which he does.

KAY
Back in the mid-fifties, the government started a little underfunded agency with the simple and laughable purpose of making contact with a race not of this planet.

As they pass an alcove, Edwards notices the six other Recruits, who have been herded into a corner. Zed, addressing them, pulls a neuralyzer from his pocket.

ZED
Now, if you'll look directly at the end of this device.

He holds a neuralyzer up in front of them, and the Recruits stare obediently at it as Zed slips on a pair of black sunglasses.

Edwards stares, fascinated, but Kay's hand reaches in and yanks him away, just as Zed's neuralyzer FLASHES WHITE.

25 INT. MIB BUILDING—HALLWAY—DAY 25

As KAY leads EDWARDS down an impossibly long corridor, he hands him a file folder stuffed thick with eight by ten photographs.

He hands Jay the first picture, a shot of eight or nine MEN in plain black suits standing around a fifties-style office with metal desks and fluorescent lights. DEE and ZED are there, much younger.

KAY
Everybody thought the agency was a joke. Except the aliens. They made contact on March 2nd, 1961, outside New York City.

Another photograph, a grainy black and white image of two ships hovering in the night sky—classic flying saucer shapes.

KAY (CONT'D)
There were nine of us that night. Seven agents. An amateur astronomer. And one poor kid who got lost on the wrong back road.

Yet another photograph, this one showing a young KAY, in a shirt and tie, holding a bouquet of flowers, staring at the open door of the landed flying saucer. ALIEN SHAPES are visible within.

EDWARDS
You brought the aliens flowers?

Kay steers Edwards to the right, down another corridor, just as long as the first.

KAY
They were intergalactic refugees with a simple request. Let us use the earth as an apolitical zone for people without a planet. Ever see "Casablanca?" Same thing, no Nazis. We agreed. So we masked all evidence of their landing.

Another picture, this one of the 1964 World's Fair grounds, still under construction. Giant models of rockets mark the Fair's theme of space travel; most prominent in the construction are two tall towers, with the flying saucers now mounted at the top of each.

EDWARDS
The 1964 World's Fair was a coverup?

KAY

Why else would we hold it in Queens?

(another hallway)

Now left. More nonhumans arrive every year. They live among us, in secret.

EDWARDS

I see. Not to change the subject, but when was your last cat-scan?

KAY

Every six months; it's company policy.

EDWARDS

Well, thanks for the very amusing morning, but I'm hopin' you'll show me where I came in? 'Cause this is where I go out.

They have stopped next to an unmarked door. Kay throws it open and steps inside.

KAY

Yeah, sure, hang on, I wanna grab a coffee while we're right here.

As Kay walks into the kitchenette, Edwards' jaw drops, his eyes widen, and he stares in wonderment—

—at THREE WORM-LIKE ALIENS standing around a water cooler. Tall, impossibly thin, most certainly not from New York, the aliens hold an animated conversation in a language that seems like a combination of Esperanto and microphone feedback.

KAY (CONT'D)

(to the aliens)

Don't tell me we've only got that powdered shit for cream again?

One of the Worm Aliens answers him in their native tongue and points to the counter.

KAY (CONT'D)

Oh.

He finds the cream sitting out on the counter where the alien indicated, dumps some in his coffee, and comes back outside, closing the door behind him. He reaches up and gently pushes Edwards' jaw up, closing his mouth.

KAY (CONT'D)

For future reference, this is a better look for you.

CUT TO:

26 OMIT 26

27 EXT. BATTERY PARK—DAY 27

EDWARDS, thrown for a major loop, sits like a zombie alongside KAY on a bench in Battery Park. Kay drinks his coffee while they talk.

KAY

Any given time, around fifteen hundred landed aliens are on the planet, the majority right here in Manhattan. Most aliens are decent enough, just trying to make a living.

EDWARDS

Cab drivers?

KAY

Not as many as you'd think. Humans, for the most part, don't have a clue. Don't want one, either. They're happy. They think they've got a pretty good bead on things.

EDWARDS

Why the big secret? People are smart, they can handle it.

KAY

A person is smart. People are dumb. Everything they've ever "known" has been proven to be wrong. A thousand years ago everybody knew as a fact, that the earth was the center of the universe. Five hundred years ago, they knew it was flat. Fifteen minutes ago, you knew we humans were alone on it. Imagine what you'll know tomorrow.

EDWARDS

So what's the catch?

KAY

What you'll gain in perspective, you'll lose in

ways you're too young to comprehend. You give up everything. Sever every human contact. No one will know you exist. Ever.

EDWARDS

Nobody?

KAY

You're not even allowed a favorite shirt. There. That's the speech I never heard. That's the choice I never got.

EDWARDS

Hold up. You track me down, put me through those stupid-ass tests, now you're trying to talk me out of it. I don't get it.

KAY

You got 'til sun-up.

EDWARDS

Is it worth it?

KAY

You find out, you let me know.

DISSOLVE TO:

28 EXT. BATTERY PARK—DUSK 28

Almost nighttime now, and the park is empty. EDWARDS is still on the bench. And still thinking. Above him, the stars are coming out.

Slowly, he looks up, into the vastness of the heavens.

DISSOLVE TO:

29 INT. GARAGE—DAY 29

The next morning. A door opens on a garage and an ORKIN MAN steps inside, carrying a tank of toxic gas. The morning light spills on an abundance of *spiders*, crawling everywhere—big ones, small ones, hundreds of them have moved in and taken over this dusty place.

The Orkin Man sighs and sets down his tank.

ORKIN MAN

Well, well, well. Movin' right in, are we? Think we own the place?

He unfurls a hose from the side of the tank.

ORKIN MAN (CONT'D)

Got a little eviction notice for you, boys.

He raises a mask to his face and unscrews the handle on the top of the tank. LETHAL GAS starts to HISS from the end of the hose.

VOICE (O.S.)

Just what exactly do you think you're doing?

The Orkin Man turns around. EDGAR stands in the doorway to the garage, staring at him disdainfully.

ORKIN MAN

(shrugs)

Takin' care of your pest problem.

EDGAR

"Pest" problem? "*Pest?*"

ORKIN MAN

Yeah. You got a hell of an infestation.

Edgar advances on him, slowly.

EDGAR

You know, I *have* noticed an infestation here. Everywhere I look, in fact. Nothing but undeveloped, unevolved, barely conscious pond scum. So convinced of their own superiority as they scurry about their short, pointless lives.

ORKIN MAN

Well—yeah. Don't you want to get rid of 'em?

EDGAR

In the worst way.

Edgar lashes out quickly, jerking the mask off the Orkin Man's face with one hand—

—and shoving the gas hose down his throat with the other.

THE ORKIN MAN'S CAR KEYS drop to the garage floor, and Edgar picks them up.

30 EXT. GARAGE—DAY 30

A six-by-ten sheet of plywood THUDS to the driveway outside the garage. EDGAR raises one end of it so it's hanging off the back end of the Orkin man's van—now it's a ramp.

He walks off and we hear that familiar SCRAPING sound again. Edgar, GRUNTING with the effort, slowly pushes his spaceship up the ramp and into the back of the Orkin truck.

CUT TO:

31 INT. MIB BUILDING—TUNNEL VENT ROOM—DAY 31

EDWARDS stands in the middle of the tunnel vent room, the same one he first came into yesterday. The elevator doors open and KAY, obviously summoned by the OLD SECURITY GUARD, stands waiting for him.

EDWARDS

One thing you gotta know right now.

Edwards walks briskly forward and gets in the elevator with Kay.

32 INT. MIB BUILDING—ELEVATOR—DAY 32

Inside the elevator, the doors WHOOSH shut, KAY turns a key in a certain floor number, and the descent begins. EDWARDS continues.

EDWARDS

All right. I'm in because there's some next-level shit going on around here, and I'm with that. Before you beam me up, there are a couple of things we need to get straight. You chose me 'cause you recognize the skills. So as of now you can cease with all of that calling me "son" or "kid" or "sport." Cool?

KAY

Cool, slick. Now about those skills of yours,

The elevator doors—

33 INT. MIB BUILDING—HEADQUARTERS—DAY 33

—slide open on Men in Black headquarters.

KAY

As of this moment, they don't mean much.

It's unlike anything we've ever seen—huge, multileveled, of sixties design, polished steel and glass. The workplaces are sleek and uncluttered, manned by both HUMANS and ALIENS. Most of the Aliens stay in the background, like the UPSIDE-DOWN GUY who walks on the ceiling, shuffling papers.

KAY and EDWARDS step off the elevator and onto a platform that looks out over the whole place.

Kay leads him down into the complex. First, they walk past a sort of passport control center, where a human BUREAUCRAT at a desk is checking the documents of a line of ALIENS who've just arrived. There are a dozen bizarre life forms in that line, CHATTING in half a dozen different alien tongues.

Edwards slows as they pass, listening to the PASSPORT CONTROL OFFICER as he addresses an ARQUILLIAN, a large, humanoid visitor.

PASSPORT OFFICER

Purpose of trip?

ARQUILLIAN

Diplomatic mission.

PASSPORT OFFICER

Duration of stay?

ARQUILLIAN

Lunch.

PASSPORT OFFICER

Carrying any fruits or vegetables?

Edwards just stares, fascinated, but Kay grabs him by the arm and hurries him along.

KAY

Let's go. He's a little...grouchy.

Kay moves him into the central hall.

KAY

A couple of hours wait after a 17-light-year flight would get on anybody's nerves.

EDWARDS

What branch of the government do we report to?

KAY

None. They started asking too many questions.

EDWARDS

So who pays for all this?

KAY

Oh, we hold a few patents on gadgets we confiscated from our out-of-state visitors. Velcro. Microwave Ovens. Liposuction.

AT A STORAGE CAGE, Kay turns a key in the lock of a caged-in area and throws the door open. Inside, there are piles of sophisticated-looking devices stacked on shelves and tabletops.

KAY

(picking something up)

Here. A new recording device to replace CD's. So now I gotta buy the White Album again?

(something else)

This is amusing. Universal translator.

He holds up a cylindrical metal tube and a small wire clip that looks like a lapel microphone.

KAY (CONT'D)

We're not supposed to have it. I'll tell you why. Human thought is so primitive it's considered an infectious disease. Makes you proud, doesn't it?

Edwards picks up a small yellow ball from one of the shelves.

EDWARDS

What's this?

KAY (CONT'D)

Don't touch that!

THE BALL *ZINGS* OUT OF EDWARDS' HANDS—it flies out into the main complex—hits the ceiling and *ricochets* around the room, faster than the eye can follow—

VARIOUS SHOTS OF HUMANS AND ALIENS ducking, dodging, and jumping out of its way.

ON KAY as he calmly, a little wearily, slips an odd-looking metal glove over his right hand...

He raises his hand and the yellow ball *zings* into it—Kay catches the ball, calmly.

KAY (CONT'D)

Caused the '77 New York blackout. Practical joke by the Great Attractor. He thought it was funny as hell.

They leave the room.

EDWARDS

Sorry!

ON THE MAIN FLOOR, they walk briskly across the room, reaching a giant screen on the far wall.

KAY

Observation, the heart of our little endeavor.

The screen displays a map of the world on which thousands of tiny lights blink in all parts of the globe, log lines of data flashing next to them.

KAY (CONT'D)

This map shows the location of every registered alien on earth at any given time. Some of them we keep under constant surveillance.

He hits a button on the console and the map is replaced by hundreds of boxes, each with smaller video images.

KAY (CONT'D)

Everyone on these screens is an alien. In public—normal. In private—you'll get the idea.

ON THE SCREENS, we see live images of aliens. Aliens who look alien are in spots where they can't be seen.

Aliens who look human are functioning right out in public—including SAM DONALDSON. MICHAEL JACKSON. And TONY ROBBINS.

KAY (CONT'D)

Meet the twins.

Kay gestures to two small, bony CREATURES with eight arms each and a single eye growing out of a central stalk in their heads. They turn around and wave two or three arms each.

EDWARDS

I gotta be honest about something.

KAY

It makes no sense?

EDWARDS

It makes perfect sense. When I was a third grader in Philadelphia, they told me I was crazy 'cause I swore that our teacher was from, like, Venus or something.

KAY

Mrs. Edelson.

Edwards, stunned, looks at Kay as 4-Eyes boots her onto the screen: Mean face, cat glasses. Bony fingers. Extremely well-hidden tail.

KAY

Jupiter, actually. Well, one of the moons.

With their remaining arms, they punch button after button on the enormous console. ZED, who was standing up close to the screen, walks over to Edwards, sizing him up.

ZED

What's your jacket size, Edwards?

EDWARDS

Uh—forty regular.

ZED

Then let's put it on.

EDWARDS

Put what on?

ZED

The last suit you'll ever wear.

CUT TO:

34 INT. MIB BUILDING—LOCKER ROOM—DAY 34

Like the rest of the place, the MIB locker room is all white. White walls, white floor, white ceiling, white lockers. ZED'S VOICE comes over:

ZED (O.S.)

From now on, you'll dress only in attire specially sanctioned by MIB Special Services.

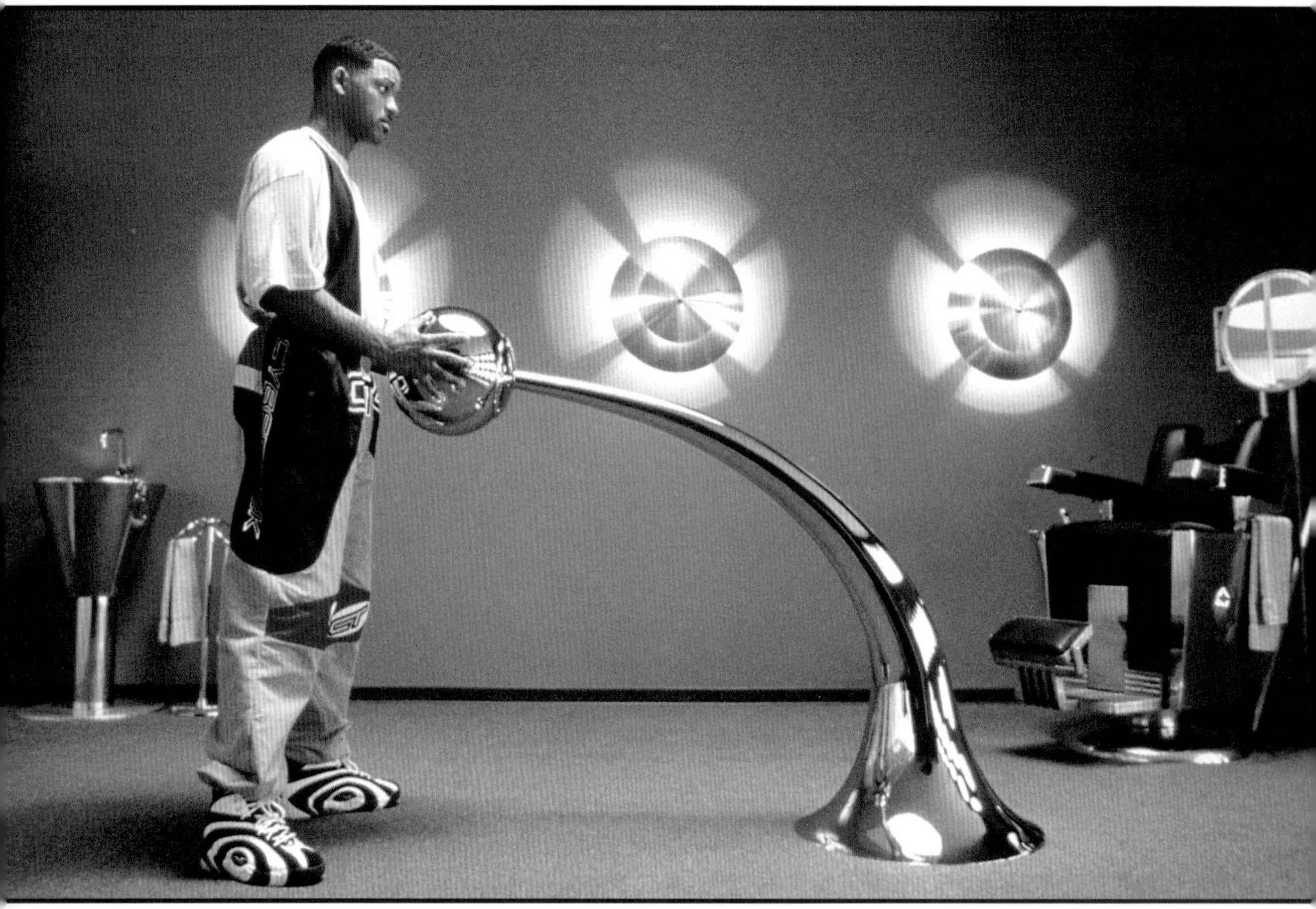

EDWARDS reaches out and opens a white locker, revealing a BLACK SUIT hung from a hanger in the middle. Above it, on the shelf, a BLACK HAT and a pair of BLACK SUNGLASSES. On the bottom, a pair of SHINY BLACK SHOES.

35 INT. MIB BUILDING—HEADQUARTERS—DAY 35

KAY is at a computer terminal. On screen are Edwards's birth certificate, driver's license, social security card, library card, everything. ZED'S VOICE continues:

ZED (O.S.)
You'll conform to the identity we give you, eat where we tell you, live where we tell you, get approval for any expenditure over a hundred dollars.

36 INT. MIB BUILDING LASER BOOTH—DAY 36

EDWARDS stands in a cramped white booth.

He holds both his hands on a TEN-FINGERED KEYPAD, pressing down hard. The pad glows red, a SEARING sound comes from his hands, and he grimaces as more lasers instantly and (not at all) painlessly change his fingerprints.

ZED (O.S.)
You will have no identifying marks of any kind. You will not stand out in any way.

37 INT. MIB BUILDING—HEADQUARTERS—DAY 37

One by one, KAY deletes Edwards's identity cards.

On the computer screen is Edwards' full name—JAMES DARREL EDWARDS III. Kay punches a couple keys, and the cursor begins to sweep from right to left, starting to eliminate the rightmost letters of Edwards's name.

ZED (O.S.)
Your entire image is carefully crafted to leave no lasting memory whatsoever with anyone you encounter.

38 INT. MIB BUILDING—LOCKER ROOM—DAY 38

Pants come off the hanger. The white shirt is removed.
More letters are eliminated from his name. It reads "JAMES DARREL ED..." then "JAMES DARR..."

ZED (O.S.)
You're a rumor, recognizable only as déja vu and dismissed just as quickly. You don't exist; you were never even born.

The coat is removed. The hat comes off the shelf.

ZED (O.S.)
Anonymity is your name. Silence your native tongue.

"JAMES..." "JAM..."

ZED (O.S.)
You are no longer part of "the system." We're above the system. Over it. Beyond it.

Feet slip into black shoes. A belt is buckled. A tie pushed up.

ZED (O.S.)
We're "them." We're "they."

On screen, all that's left is the letter "J."
As the coat is buttoned, we notice the sleeve. Monogrammed on the cuff is, simply, the letter "J."

ZED (O.S.)
We are the Men in Black.

39 INT. MIB BUILDING—HEADQUARTERS—DAY 39

Looking slick and handsome in his extremely sharp suit, JAMES D EDWARDS III—or, rather, JAY—steps into the doorway from the locker room. He reaches into his pocket, takes out the sunglasses, and looks at KAY.

JAY
The difference between you and me?

He slips on the sunglasses.

JAY (CONT'D)
I make this look good.

CUT TO:

A39 EXT. NEW JERSEY—EARLY MORNING A39

We are looking at a telephoto shot of Manhattan in all its splendor.
We see the Orkin van topping a hill, heading towards Manhattan.

40 INT. MIB BUILDING—ZED'S OFFICE—DAY 40

Zed's office is a circular, windowed room elevated above the main floor of MIB headquarters. JAY and KAY sit across the desk from Zed. There are five video monitors on a wall behind Zed's desk, and on each monitor is another Man in Black, in different parts of the world, the city name and a clock ticking in a corner of the image.
While Zed talks, he goes through paperwork on his desk.

ZED
Okay, let's see.
(to one of the monitors)
Bee, we got the deposed sur-prefect of Sinalee touching down in the forest outside Portland tonight. I'm pulling you down from Anchorage to do a meet-and-greet.

BEE, an agent on one of the monitors, nods.

BEE
Humanoid?

ZED
You wish. Bring a sponge.
(going through memos)
What else—everybody, we gotta keep Rolling Fish-Goat out of the sewer system, he's scaring the rats. And Bobo the Squat wants to reveal himself on "Unsolved Mysteries." Bee, make sure he doesn't.

He turns a page, coming across a red memo.

ZED (CONT'D)
Red-letter from last night—we had an unauthorized landing somewhere in upstate New York farm country. Keep your ears open for this one, Kay, we're not hosting a galactic kegger down here.

Next to him, his computer screen BEEPS importantly. Zed looks over at it.

ZED
Well, well, well—we got a skimmer.

KAY
(to Jay)
Landed alien out of zone.
(to Zed)
Who is it?

ZED
Redgick. He's not cleared to leave Manhattan but he's way out of town right now, stuck in traffic on the New Jersey Turnpike. Why don't you take Jay? This is a good one for him to warm up on.

41 EXT. MIB BUILDING—BATTERY PARK—DAY 41

JAY and KAY come out the front of MIB headquarters.

JAY

Yo, wussup with Zed?

(imitating him)

"Go get em, tiger. We're not hosting an intergalactic kegger..."

KAY

Zed was saving the world before you were born, son. Show some respect.

An MIB MECHANIC pulls up in Kay's black LTD and hops out, leaving the door open. Jay sizes up the car.

JAY

We got the use of unlimited technology from the entire universe and we cruise around in this?

Kay glares at Jay. He's getting annoyed.

42 INT. MIB LTD—DAY 42

They get in and slam the doors. Kay starts the car and the engine HUMS quietly.

KAY

Seat belt.

JAY

You know, ya'll gotta learn how to talk to people. You could be a little kinder and gentler.

Kay grits his teeth.

KAY

Buckle up, please.

JAY

Now did that hurt?

Kay shifts the car into reverse. The awesome power of the car kicks in and Jay sails forward, THWACKING into the dash. Kay shifts into forward and taps the gas, SLAMMING Jay back into his seat.

KAY

Makin' fun of my ride...

A LIGHTED PANEL rotates into place between the two front seats. Jay's hand falls by accident on a flashing red button in the panel.

KAY

Jay. The button?

JAY

Yeah?

KAY

Never push the button, Jay.

Jay jerks his hand away.

CUT TO:

43 EXT. HIGHWAY—SIDE OF THE ROAD—DAY 43

The LTD is now stopped by the side of the road, dust swirling around it. Ahead of it, another car has pulled over. KAY gets out, JAY follows a moment later, shaky-legged. Kay walks up to the window of the car they've stopped. The DRIVER, a guy in his mid-thirties with a WIFE in her mid-thirties, rolls the window down.

KAY

License and registration, please.

The Driver hands over some documents. Kay flips through them.

KAY (CONT'D)

Other license and registration, please.

The guy digs out two other cards and hands those over. Jay peers over Kay's shoulder.

The photographs on the "RESIDENT ALIEN ID" cards are of two friendly-looking reptile types, husband and wife, smiling at the camera, their long, skinny tongues dangling in a friendly sort of way.

Kay hands them back.

KAY (CONT'D)
Your resident card has you restricted to the five boroughs only. Where do you think you're going?

REDGICK
It's my wife! She's— she's— well, *look!*

Kay leans down and looks in the window. MRS. REDGICK is in front, MOANING in pain, holding her swollen belly. Kay straightens up, fast.

KAY
Oh God. How soon?

Mrs. Redgick SCREAMS in pain. Real soon. For the first time since we've seen him, Kay is nervous.

KAY (CONT'D)
Okay. All right. No big deal.
(to Jay)
You handle it.

JAY
Me?

KAY
Sure, it's easy, you just sorta—catch.

Mrs. Redgick SCREAMS again. Redgick gets out of the car, worried.

REDGICK
Are you sure he knows what he's doing?

KAY
Yeah, hell, sure, he does this all the time. C'mon, let him work, Redgick, I wanna ask you something.

Kay gives Jay a supportive SLAP on the back and leads Redgick away, to the rear of the car. Jay stays in the background and opens the rear door, tentatively. He leans down, into the car.

JAY
Oh God! I see it I see it I see it!

A few yards from the car, Kay turns Redgick to face him.

KAY
Croagg the Midwife's back on 64th and 8th. You were headed *out* of town.

REDGICK
Well, we're, uh—meeting someone.

Suddenly a TENTACLE whips out from between Mrs. Redgick's legs, CRACKS the whip once, and wraps around the door post, grabbing hold.

JAY
Oh sweet Jesus Mother of God did you see that?!

KAY
(still to Redgick)
So? Who you meeting?

REDGICK
Well, it's—a ship.

KAY
Really? I didn't see a departure clearance for today.

REDGICK
You didn't? Uh, well—it was an emergency.

Now a SECOND TENTACLE whips out, but this one wraps around *Jay's neck* and pulls tight. He GASPS, choking.

JAY
Guys— guys—

KAY
Doin' fine, Ace.
(back to Redgick)
What kind of emergency? What's the rush to get off the planet all of a sudden?

JAY
(choking to death)
Help?! HELP! Hello?!

He starts tugging for all he's worth, but the fight is sort of going against him, as the tentacles pull him in even harder than he tries to pull the baby *out.*

REDGICK
We just don't like the neighborhood anymore. Some of the—new arrivals.

Redgick looks at Kay, clearly concealing something, but darts his eyes away.

KAY
What new arrivals? This have anything to do with the crasher from last night?

JAY
(Screaming)
Can you guys do this later?!

But in that moment, Jay finally gets a foot up on the door frame, acquires leverage, and RIPS the baby free. He falls, flat on his back in the dirt, the *multi-tentacled lizardlike baby* resting squarely on his chest.

JAY (CONT'D)
Oh— oh— oh— man.

Kay turns and claps Redgick on the back.

KAY

Congratulations! It's a lizard.

Jay looks down at the creature COOING and nestling on his chest.

JAY

(misty)

Hey, you know, it *is* sorta—

It vomits on him.

CUT TO:

44 EXT. HIGHWAY—SIDE OF THE ROAD—MIB LTD—DAY 44

Back in the car, JAY wipes the last of the puke off his suit while KAY starts up the car.

KAY

Anything about that seem unusual to you?

Jay just looks at him, very Jack Benny.

JAY

Pick.

KAY

What kind of "new arrival" would scare Redgick so bad that he'd risk a warp jump with a newborn?

(thinks)

Let's check the hot sheets.

45 EXT. NEWSSTAND—DAY 45

CLOSE ON on various supermarket tabloids as a hand flips through them. There are headlines like "POPE A FATHER!"and "TOP DOCTORS BAFFLED—BABY BORN PREGNANT!" and "MAN EATS OWN HOUSE!" (the subhead on that one is "And That's Just the Appetizer, Says Neighbor.")

KAY and JAY are at a downtown newsstand. Kay is furiously searching through the tabs; Jay is standing behind him, a little embarrassed.

JAY

These are the hot sheets?

Kay pulls a copy of the *Weekly World News* from the stand and gives the guy a buck.

KAY

Best damn investigative reporting on the planet. But hey, go ahead, read the *New York Times* if you want. They get lucky sometimes.

JAY

You're actually looking for tips in a supermarket tabloid?

KAY

Not looking for. *Found.*

He SMACKS the paper down on the hood in front of Jay, the pages turned open to a headline in typeface so large one would think it reserved for the Second Coming:

Farm wife says
"ALIEN STOLE MY HUSBAND'S SKIN!"

CUT TO:

46 EXT. GEM AND JEWELRY STORE—ORKIN VAN—DAY 46

A flap of skin, now getting gray and crusty with age, hangs off EDGAR's neck as he sits in the front of his Orkin van. He sucks as hard as he possibly can on a straw stuck into a Jolt Cola ("Double the Sugar! Triple the Caffeine!"), one of a six-pack that sits on the dashboard.

Across the street, Edgar sees a short, older man come out of one of the jewelry shops on Thirty-Fifth Street. Edgar drops the soda and stares.

The Older Man (ROSENBERG), is carrying a cat and an ornate rosewood jewelry box. Carefully, he sets the box down and lovingly places the cat on top of it while he locks all five locks on the door to his distinctive shop.

That finished, he picks up the cat, then the box, then waddles off down the street, one under each arm.

Edgar drops the truck into gear and follows him, slowly, trolling along behind him.

ON THE STREET, Rosenberg walks happily along, HUMMING to himself. He gives his cat a little peck. As he rounds a corner, we recognize the tune he's humming—"I've Got the Whole World In My Hands."

The Orkin van rounds the corner behind him. Following.

CUT TO:

47 EXT. FARMHOUSE—DAY 47

The LTD pulls to a stop at the end of the driveway that leads to Beatrice's farmhouse, where the alien ship landed. The wrecked pickup truck is still there. JAY and KAY get out, very undercover cop. Jay starts up the driveway.

KAY

Not so fast. Walk up slow.

JAY

Why?

KAY

Part of the routine. Makes it look like we're sizing up the situation. Gives her time to get the wrong impression.

BEATRICE appears in the door to the house, curious.

KAY (CONT'D)

Puts some fear into her. Makes things go smoother.

Beatrice calls to them.

BEATRICE

Can I help you gentlemen?

Beatrice looks much better than the last time we saw her—more nicely dressed, a touch of makeup, a smile on her face.

Kay pulls a black card from his wallet and extends it to her as she draws close. As she reaches for it, the card reforms into an FBI badge.

KAY

How do you do, ma'am, I'm Special Agent Manheim, this is Agent Black, FBI. Had a few questions about your visitor.

BEATRICE

Are you here to make fun of me too?

KAY

No ma'am. We at the FBI don't have a sense of humor that we're aware of. Mind if we come in?

BEATRICE

Sure. Lemonade?

CUT TO:

48 INT. FARMHOUSE—LIVING ROOM—DAY 48

In the living room, KAY sips some of her lemonade and winces. JAY moves through the room, checking it out as BEATRICE tells her story.

BEATRICE

And *they* said to me, "If he was murdered, how could he walk back in the house?" And I must admit, I was a little stumped by that one. But I know Edgar. And that wasn't him. It was more like something *else* that was *wearing* him. Like a suit. An Edgar suit.

A little GIGGLE escapes her at the thought. Jay, over by a bookcase, notices a framed PHOTO OF EDGAR, kneeling in the woods, proudly about to skin a deer.

JAY

Damn. If he was this ugly *before* he was an alien...

BEATRICE

Sorry?

KAY

Go on.

BEATRICE

Anyway, when I came to, he was gone.

KAY

Did he say anything?

BEATRICE

Yes! He asked for water. Sugar water, if I remember.

KAY

Sugar water.

JAY

Did you taste her lemonade?

Kay nods, puts on his sunglasses. Takes out another pair, hands them to Jay.

Kay draws his neuralyzer. FLASH! Beatrice freezes, staring straight ahead as if hypnotized. Kay takes Jay's glasses off and hands them back to him.

KAY

Ray Bans.

(pulling off Jay's sunglasses)

Okay, Beatrice. There was no alien, and the flash of light you saw in the sky wasn't a UFO. Swamp gas from a weather balloon was trapped in a thermal pocket and refracted the light from Venus—

JAY

Whoa! That thing erases her memory, and you give her a new one?

KAY

Standard issue neuralyzer.

JAY

And that's the best you can come up with?

KAY

On a more personal note, Beatrice, Edgar ran off with on old girlfriend. Go stay at your mother's for a few days and get over it. Decide you're better off.

JAY

(butting in)

Yeah, and you're better off 'cause he never appreciated you anyway. In fact, you kicked *him* out, and now that he's gone, you ought to buy some new clothes, maybe hire a decorator or something...

CUT TO:

49 EXT. FARMHOUSE—DAY 49

KAY is in the hole where the ship landed, investigating.

He holds a pocket spectral analyzer over a section of scorched earth. The analyzer shifts colors. Red. Then Yellow.

JAY
(from up outside the hole)
Hey. Kay...when am I gonna get one of those memory things?

The spectral analyzer turns blue.

KAY
When you're ready.
(re: analyzer)
Please—not green.

Purple. *And then green.*

Kay closes his eyes and sits back, leaning against the dirt. Above him, JAY leans over, staring down. Kay looks up at him.

KAY (CONT'D)
Do you know what alien life form leaves a green spectral trail?

JAY
Wait—don't tell me—that was the question on Final Jeopardy last night.

AT THE CAR, Kay snatches up the radio handset and keys the microphone.

KAY
(softly, into mic)
Zed, we have a bug.

He turns off the radio and sighs. Jay stands next to him.

JAY
I'm gonna jump way past you and just guess that this is bad. Right?

KAY
Bugs thrive on carnage, Tiger. They consume, infest and destroy. They live off the death and decay of other species.

JAY
So basically you have a racial problem with all insect-based life forms?

KAY
Listen, kid—imagine a giant cockroach five times smarter than Albert Einstein, four times stronger than an ox, nine times meaner than hell, strutting his stuff around Manhattan Island in his brand new Edgar suit. Does that sound like fun?

JAY
What do we do?

KAY
With a bug in town? Watch the morgues.

CUT TO:

50 OMIT 50

51 EXT. LESHKO'S DINER—DAY 51

ROSENBERG, the jewelry store owner, steps out of a cab in the meat-packing district, still carrying the ornate box and his beloved cat. He heads into Leshko's, a Russian diner.

A moment later, the Orkin van pulls to a stop across the street.

52 INT. LESHKO'S DINER—DAY 52

ROSENBERG comes into the tiny restaurant, squinting in the relative darkness. At a table in the middle, he sees a man eating alone—an enormous, dignified, yet profoundly strange-looking man in his mid-fifties.

Rosenberg walks carefully over to the table, but does not sit down. The man (an ARQUILLIAN, and if we're eagle-eyed, we recognize him as the alien on a "diplomatic mission" from passport control) rises from his chair. He steps forward, to face Rosenberg, who sets the ornate box on the table. Immediately, ROSENBERG'S CAT jumps on top of it.

Rosenberg and the Arquillian stare at each other for a long moment—

—and then embrace each other. The embrace has an odd, formal quality to it, like mafiosi coming to a sit-down. They hold on, long and hard, and both seemed choked with emotion.

Finally, they break apart and take their seats. They speak in a bizarre alien tongue, which is **subtitled.** Rosenberg wipes away tears.

ROSENBERG
Sorry I'm late. The cab drivers on this planet are terrible.

ARQUILLIAN
Your majesty, you are in grave danger.

ROSENBERG
Yeah, and they overcharge you every time.

ARQUILLIAN
Sir, a bug landed here. We must get you off the planet.

ROSENBERG
A bug? He must know why I'm here.

ARQUILLIAN
We think he does.
(noticing the ornate box on the table)
Is that what I think it is?

ROSENBERG

No, just some diamonds for your children. Do we have time to eat?

The Arquillian relaxes.

ARQUILLIAN

Sure. I ordered you some pirogi.

53 INT. LESHKO'S DINER—KITCHEN—DAY 53

In the kitchen, the Russian COOK slaps two orders of pirogi up on the stainless steel counter —

COOK

Table six is up!

—and turns away, back to the grill.

A HAND reaches in, takes the plates, and sets them on a tray. We follow the tray, but see only the right arm and aproned midsection of the waiter carrying it. He carries the tray along the counter toward a pair of swinging doors that lead out into the restaurant.

The doors swing in as another WAITER sweeps into the kitchen, and our waiter heads out into the dining area. As the doors swing closed behind him, they reveal storage shelves crammed with bags of rice, cans of stewed tomatoes—

—and a DEAD WAITER, literally folded in half and stuffed in among the shelves.

54 INT. LESHKO'S DINER—DAY 54

ROSENBERG and the ARQUILLIAN raise their glasses in a toast.

ARQUILLIAN

To the continued reign of the Arquillian Empire.

ROSENBERG

To the safety of the galaxy.

They CLINK glasses and drink, just as the Waiter arrives. Still, we see only his arms and midsection as he sets the tray on a stand and lifts the plates of pirogi. He carries them to the table and sets them down.

Rosenberg, setting his glass down next to the plate, catches a glimpse of the Waiter's hand—

—just as an enormous *silverfish* bug slithers out of the waiter's sleeve and scurries across the table. The glass slips out of Rosenberg's hand, dumping wine all over the table.

He looks up, slowly, and sees the Waiter's face.

It's EDGAR. Another half dozen insects of all variety tumble out of Edgar's sleeves and scurry across the table. Rosenberg and the Arquillian freeze, paralyzed with fear. They seem to know what dire implications Edgar's presence holds.

ROSENBERG

(in English again)

You can kill us both—but you will not find it.

Edgar smiles.

EDGAR

You're right about one thing.

Suddenly a long STINGER whips out from under the back of Edgar's apron and zips under the table. First Rosenberg and then the Arquillian lurch forward their chairs, their faces contorting in pain.

They both pitch forward, their faces slogging into fresh pirogi.

The stinger SNAPS out from under the table and whips back under Edgar's apron. He moves quickly, searching their pockets, but he doesn't find what he's looking for. The cat, still perched on top of the ornate box, HISSES at him.

Edgar reaches out and BATS the cat away with one vicious swipe of his hand. The animal HOWLS and flies across the room, landing in a WOMAN's lunch.

The Woman SCREAMS. Now other DINERS' attention is drawn to Edgar's table, where two obviously dead men are being robbed by a waiter. There are SHOUTS of outrage, a few MEN rise out of their seats.

Edgar grabs the ornate box and tries to open it, but finds it locked. With the furor rising around him, he shoves the box under one arm and bolts for the door.

Rosenberg's cat leaps back onto the table and SNARLS at him as he goes.

CUT TO:

55 EXT. LESHKO'S DINER—DAY 55

Later, and the Russian diner is now a crime scene, clustered with COPS and flashing lights. THREE BODIES, now on stretchers and covered with sheets, are being loaded into the back of ambulances.

ROSENBERG'S CAT races out of a UNIFORMED COP's arms and leaps onto one of the stretchers, MEOWING mournfully. The Uniformed Cop turns to a POLICE INSPECTOR who is questioning the WOMAN from the diner.

COP

What am I supposed to do with the cat?

INSPECTOR

I don't know. Send it with the stiff. Let family claim it.

The Cop nods and follows the stretcher with Rosenberg's body into the back of one of the ambulances, allowing the cat to ride on the chest of its dead owner for the time being.

The doors of the wagon SLAM shut.

CUT TO:

56 INT. MORGUE—CORRIDOR—DAY 56

The stretcher with the corpse on it is wheeled down a corridor in police headquarters. ROSENBERG'S CAT, still on his chest, MEOWS curiously as the stretcher approaches two doors with "City Morgue" written across them. The words split in half as the stretcher BANGS through the doors.

57 INT. MORGUE—DAY 57

The city morgue is a crowded, brightly-lit, tiled place with corpses parked left and right. Busy day in the Apple. The Cop wheeling the stretcher calls out to the CORONER, who's hunched over another body.

COP

Where do you want contestant number three?

The coroner turns around. It's DR. LAUREL WEAVER, the woman who tried to speak to Jay before. She sighs and waves a hand.

LAUREL

By the wall, I guess.

(noticing)

What's with the cat?

COP

Oh, the cat. There's a problem with the cat. Sign here.

Laurel signs his clipboard.

LAUREL

What's the problem with the cat?

COP

Your problem.

Laurel gives him a dirty look, but he laughs and leaves. She goes over to the stretcher and bends down, petting Rosenberg's cat gently.

LAUREL

Are you having a bad day, baby? Cheer up.

(of Rosenberg)

His is worse.

She sets the cat aside and wheels the stretcher under the lights.

LAUREL (CONT'D)

Okey-dokey. Shall we?

58 INT. MORGUE—LATER—DAY 58

Laurel is hunched over the corpse, the only light in the room coming from the overhead spot that illuminates her work.

Fascinated by something, she digs deeper. And deeper. And looks up, her face a mixture of alarm and excitement.

LAUREL

Oh, my God.

CUT TO:

59 EXT. MORGUE—NIGHT 59

Kay's LTD pulls up in front of the morgue.

60 INT. MORGUE—CORRIDOR—NIGHT 60

Two men in black suits hurry down the stairs and into the corridor outside the morgue. They hasten down the hallway, their shoes CLICKING in perfect lockstep, headed for those swinging doors at the other end.

JAY and KAY. Men in Black on a mission.

61 INT. MORGUE—NIGHT 61

In the morgue, LAUREL has fallen asleep on her desk, her head in her arms. ROSENBERG'S CAT sits on the desk next to her, licking its paws. Suddenly, the cat looks up, MEOWING urgently.

Laurel looks up and, following the cat's gaze, turns around slowly in her chair. JAY and KAY stand in the doorway, staring at her. Kay steps forward, holding out that black card again. It reforms into another kind of official ID, this time it says "DEPARTMENT OF PUBLIC HEALTH"

LAUREL

(into recorder)

...approximately 112 degrees at time of autopsy, indicating, quite impossibly, a post-mortem
increase in body temperature. Examiner attempted to verify result rectally, only to find subject was, uh, without rectum. Which can only be
described as...well...as really...

KAY (O.S.)

Weird? Dr. Leo Menville, Department of Public Health. This is Dr. White.

She looks up. Jay and Kay are standing there.

LAUREL

Yeah, well whoever you are, I'm afraid I'm going to need to see some ID.

He hands her his CARTE NOIR, which changes to read "Dr. Menville, Department of Public Health." She hands it back.

LAUREL

(checking her watch)

You boys must not have much of a home life.

KAY

We watch the morgues very carefully. You've got something unusual?

LAUREL

I'd say so—triple homicide.

She gets up and goes to the Arquillian's body, which is still out on a table under the lights.

LAUREL (CONT'D)

The first corpse was perfectly normal, except that he was broken in half, but when I opened up the other two—well, look.

She throws back a sheet, revealing (to them only, not us)

the fully dissected Arquillian. Kay raises an eyebrow; Jay nearly retches.

LAUREL (CONT'D)

There's a skeletal structure at work here unlike anything I've ever seen.

Kay steps past her, going straight to the body. He begins to examine it.

KAY

I'll have a look at this one. Dr. White, why don't you and Dr. Weaver check out the other body?

LAUREL

This way, Doctor.

Jay and Laurel cross the room, to where ROSENBERG's corpse lies out on another gurney.

LAUREL (CONT'D)

This one's even stranger. I did a full laparotomy. I started with the lesser curvature of the stomach—though, if you want, we could begin at the gastro-esophageal junction.

JAY

I think, uh, we should start at the same place you did.

LAUREL

All right.

Jay hears a MEOW and looks down. Rosenberg's cat is rubbing up against his leg.

JAY

Your cat?

LAUREL

Guess it is now. Came in with the bodies.

She SNAPS one of her rubber gloves and reaches down (out of frame), sinking her hands into the body as she moves things aside. Just by the look on Jay's face, one can imagine how disgusting it is.

Laurel digs in, up to her elbows. Jay winces. She pulls one bloody glove out, to wipe a strand of hair out of her face. He looks at her—

—and she *winks* at him. He's surprised. She laughs.

LAUREL (CONT'D)

Okay. Dive right in. God knows he won't mind.

Jay is reluctant, so she rolls her eyes and helps him, taking him by the hand and guiding him into the thick of the corpse.

LAUREL (CONT'D)

You have very pretty eyes.

JAY

Thank-you, but is this really the time to uh—you know, come on to me?

LAUREL

Hey, just walking the dog.

(continuing)

Feel that? Where the piloric junction would be?

JAY

Oh, yes. Exactly.

LAUREL

Now push that aside. Notice anything strange? Stomach? Liver? Lungs?

JAY

Nope. All fine.

LAUREL

Doctor, they're all *missing*.

JAY

(quickly)

Well, of course they are. What I'm pointing out is that there are no pieces of them left. So they're intact, wherever they are. That we can be sure of.

LAUREL

Have we met before? I have the strangest feeling of déja vu.

JAY

You know, I was just going to ask you the same thing.

Laurel looks at him sideways, skeptical, but also intrigued. She whispers to him. Confiding in him.

LAUREL

Okay. You wanna know what I really think?

(re: Kay)

But don't tell that guy. He looks like he's already under enough stress.

(then)

This body is not really a body, but it's actually some sort of transport unit for something else altogether. The question is: what?

Jay just looks at her intrigued.

LAUREL

By the way, stop me if I'm freaking you out.

JAY

No, no...not at all.

After a particularly gross GUSHY sound, he looks away, toward her. She's staring at him.

Laurel leans over and lowers her voice, just for him.

LAUREL

You know what I like to do sometimes? When it's *really* late?

JAY

(freaked out)

No...

From the other side of the room, Kay CLEARS HIS THROAT.

JAY (CONT'D)

Excuse me.

He walks across the morgue to Kay, who is still examining the Arquillian. But Jay never takes his eyes off Laurel.

KAY

What do you think?

JAY

(of Laurel)

Very interesting. Got a real Queen of the Undead thing goin' on.

KAY

Of the body.

JAY

Great body.

KAY

The *dead* body?

JAY

Not a clue.

KAY

All right. Keep her occupied. Try not to sound too dumb.

ACROSS THE MORGUE, Laurel is still examining Rosenberg, now bent down next to his head, carefully studying his left ear. She notices something strange, turns, and calls over her shoulder to Jay.

LAUREL

Dr. White.

Jay, in conversation with Kay, does not respond to what is not his name.

LAUREL (CONT'D)

(louder)

Dr. White.

(still louder)

Dr. White.

He still doesn't answer.

LAUREL (CONT'D)

(shouting)

DR. WHITE!

Kay nudges Jay.

KAY

You're up, Slugger.

Jay turns and races across the room to rejoin her.

LAUREL

Look at this.

Jay leans down. There is strange stitching around the base of Rosenberg's ear.

JAY

What is that?

He reaches out, touches the ear, then he actually turns it. With a soft CLICK—

—it pulls away from the head. Like a latch.

Jay and Laurel look at each other, astonished. Jay pulls again, and Rosenberg's entire face PUSHES OUT with a mechanical HUM, then HINGES OPEN, the whole face rotating out away from the rest of the artificial skull.

A TINY LITTLE GREEN MAN SITS INSIDE ROSENBERG'S HEAD.

Though not quite dead, the Tiny Little Green Man is gravely wounded. He staggers up out of a small control room inside Rosenberg's head, with gearshifts and viewing screens all around the inside of the skull.

LAUREL

Far—freaking—out.

They lean in closer. The Tiny Little Green Man (a BALT-

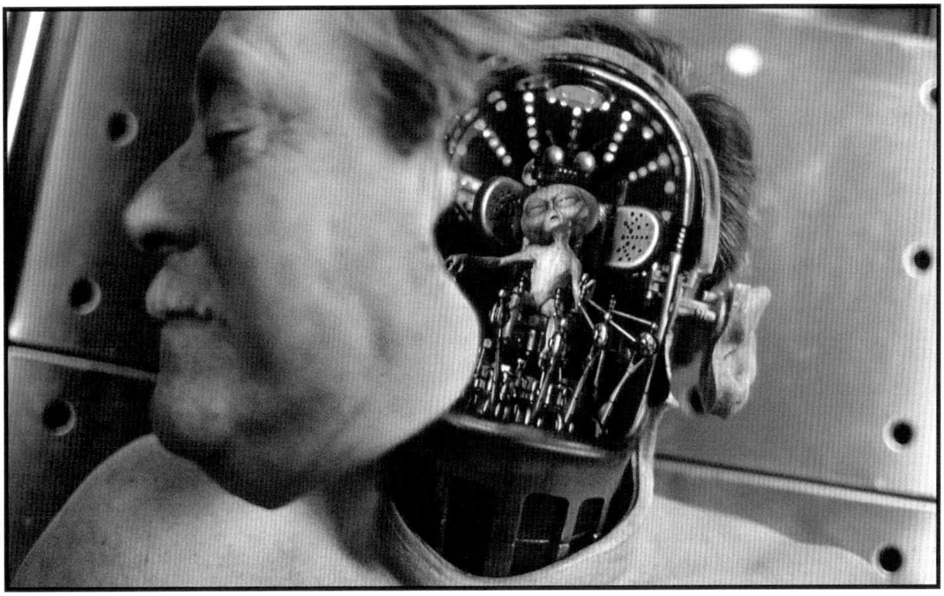

IAN) forces words out of his mouth.

BALTIAN

Must—to pre— prevent—
(searching for the word)
—contest? No...to prevent—

JAY

It's all right—What are you trying to say? Struggle?

LAUREL

War?

The Baltian nods vigorously. That's it.

BALTIAN
(faltering)

Galaxy on— or— or— Orion's—
(thinks)
What is word? Be...?

JAY

Bed? Belt? Orion's Belt?

The Baltian nods again, falls, and dies. Jay and Laurel look at the little dead alien, then at each other.

JAY (CONT'D)

"To prevent war, the galaxy is on Orion's Belt?" The hell does that mean?
(turns around)
Hey! Kay! I mean, Dr., uh, whatever, come here!

Kay begins over. Laurel looks at them.

LAUREL

"Doctor Whatever"? You're not with the Department of Public Health, are you?

Jay shakes his head—but is now paying more attention to Kay, as he leads him toward the Little Man.

JAY

He's dead.

Kay looks at the mess—the body, the little dead man.

KAY

Rosenberg. Damn. Good man.

JAY

You knew him?

KAY

One of the few I actually liked. Exiled High Prince.

LAUREL

I was right—this is an alien life form, and you're from some government agency who wants to keep it under wraps...

Kay and Jay are not paying attention to Laurel.

JAY

He said "to prevent war, the galaxy is on Orion's Belt."

LAUREL

...This make total sense. How else do you explain New York? The other night I'm in a cab, this guy...

FLASH! Without even looking at her, Kay whips out his neuralyzer and blanks her out.

KAY

He said there's a galaxy on Orion's Belt? That

makes no sense.

JAY

That's what he said.

(to the dazed Laurel)

Didn't he? Right after he—

(realizing)

Oh, for Christ's sake, you did the flashy thing already.

LAUREL

(as if awakening)

Uh, hi, whoever you guys are, I'm afraid I'm going to need to see some ID if you're going to be in the morgue, okay?

KAY

Sure thing, sweetheart. Here you go.

FLASH! He neuralyzes her again. Jay slaps his hand.

JAY

Stop that—

KAY

(to Laurel, ignoring Jay)

Typical day, too much caffeine, get a life.

JAY

—that thing probably gives you brain cancer!

KAY

Never hurt her before.

JAY

"Never hurt her before"?! How many times have you done the flashy thing to this poor woman?!

KAY

(evasive)

Couple.

JAY

Aren't you worried about, you know, long term damage?

KAY

(more evasive)

Little bit.

JAY

What the hell happened to make you such a callous son of a bitch?

KAY

I took this job.

He heads out. Jay follows.

JAY

Hey, you never flashed *me* with that thing, did you?

KAY

Nah.

A61 EXT. MORGUE—NIGHT A61

Jay and Kay exit the morgue and walk towards their car.

JAY

Hey, Kay, I really think I should be in charge of the flashy memory thing department.

KAY

Not while I'm around, Slim.

JAY

Yeah, well you're a menace with that thing...

An MIB containment vehicle pulls up, and four men dressed in black suits get out.

KAY

(to an MIB Agent)

We've got two dead aliens in there, and a deputy medical coroner in need of a new memory.

CUT TO:

62 EXT. NEW YORK ALLEY—NIGHT 62

The Orkin van is parked in an alleyway somewhere downtown. From inside, throaty WAILS of frustration can be heard. Two PASSERSBY hear the racket and hesitate, wondering if they should get involved.

But an inhuman GROWL rattles the whole van and they wise up, hurrying on their way.

63 INT. ORKIN VAN—NEW YORK ALLEY—NIGHT 63

Inside the van, the ornate rosewood box is now battered and scarred, its various locks holding tight against EDGAR's repeated attempts to claw his way into it. Crammed into the back of the van along with his spaceship, Edgar wedges a screwdriver into the thin opening between the top and the rest of the box and SMACKS it with his right fist.
Nothing doing.

He BELLOWS in rage and hurls the box against the side of the van, where it finally CRACKS a hinge. Edgar snaps it up, pries the rest of the hinge off with the screwdriver, and wrenches the top off the box.

Inside, there are dozens of precious, glittering diamonds, which he promptly tosses aside as worthless. But the rest of the box is empty.

EDGAR

No. No, NO, *NO*, **NOOOO!**

He rips the box apart with his bare hands. There's nothing else there.

CUT TO:

A63 EXT. MIB BUILDING—MAGIC HOUR A63

As lower Manhattan is waking up, Jay and Kay enter the building.

64 INT. MIB BUILDING—HEADQUARTERS—EARLY MORNING 64

Despite the early hour, the headquarters is going full- blast. The large screen displays the familiar grouping of stars that is the CONSTELLATION ORION.

Jay and Kay hurry in—Kay peels off to one of the monitors; Jay heads for Zed.

JAY

Doesn't anybody believe in sleep around here?

ZED

The twins keep us on Alpha Centaurian time—a 37-hour day. Give it a few months—you'll get used to it. Or you'll have a psychotic episode.

He points up at the screen with a laser pencil.

ZED

Here's Orion; the brightest grouping of stars in the northern sky...

(pointing)

and here's Orion's belt—

He indicates the three stars that make up the belt.

JAY

That's what the little guy was talking about, "To prevent war, the galaxy's on Orion's belt..."

ZED

There *are no* galaxies on Orion's belt. The belt is just these three *stars;* galaxies are *huge,* made up of *billions* of stars.

(switches off the laser pointer)

You heard wrong.

JAY

You're attracted to me, aren't you?

Jay starts to cross over to ANOTHER MONITOR, where Kay is sitting alone, tie loosened, slightly disheveled. On the screen, the word "SEARCHING" blinks, encouraging patience. The image changes to a satellite view of North America, which quickly zooms in on the Southwest.

On screen, the satellite view zooms down to Arizona, then a city, then a neighborhood, then a block, then a back yard. The printout changes to "SUBJECT ACQUIRED."

The image comes into sharp focus on one back yard in particular, where we get a good look at a MIDDLE-AGED WOMAN.

SUBJECT: ELIZABETH ANN RESTON
PRESENT LOCATION: RESIDENCE
553 FAIRFIELD AVE./TEMPE/AZ

Whoever Elizabeth Ann Reston is, she's lovely. She's setting a picnic table in her back yard at the moment, unaware that she's being watched by an eye in the sky—just as Kay is unaware that Jay is standing behind him.

Jay notices the monitor with the Middle-aged Woman on it. He looks at Kay's expression, then back at the monitor.

JAY

Pretty lady...

Kay clicks off the picture of her. Jay drags a chair and sits down.

JAY (CONT'D)

You were the guy with the flowers in the photo, (the night the aliens arrived.) [What, you were on your way to a dance or something and you got lost? And she never got those flowers, did she?]

Kay doesn't answer, just stares at the screen. Elizabeth looks up, as if she knows she's being watched, but she's just looking at the sky, wondering how many stars'll be out tonight.

JAY (CONT'D)

Grumpy Guy's story comes into focus. She ever get married?

KAY

No.

It's more than Kay can bear. He reaches out and flicks a switch. The monitor goes blank, except for a data screen:

SUBJECT LOST

Kay sits back in the chair and eats a potato chip morosely. Jay looks at him: "Is this me in thirty years?" A moment goes by. Finally:

JAY

Well, it's better to have loved and lost than never to have—

KAY

Try it.

ZED (O.S.)

Kay.

Jay and Kay cross back toward the LAD (Landed Alien Display), where each of the thousand or so Aliens who live on earth are represented by a flickering LIGHT.

Some lights are starting to go out.

KAY

(quietly, with dread)

They're leaving.

ZED

We've had twelve jumps in the last hour. Redgick was just the beginning.

JAY

What do they know that we don't know?

Kay looks to his partner, then to the screen. Another light flickers out.

KAY

Why do rats desert the ship?

(to the twins)

Go to Lem Sat IV. Put up a forty-field view of Manhattan.

ON THE SCREEN New York City is just a bright spot of light on the Eastern coast of the United States.

KAY (CONT'D)

Four hundred.

Now there's a view of the earth from space. Nothing unusual.

KAY (CONT'D)

Four thousand.

Now we're looking at earth from far, far away—and from here we can see something that doesn't belong in this picture:

A BATTLE CRUISER far off to one side of the earth. The words "LEVEL FOUR" flash in red letters on one side of the map.

KAY (CONT'D)

That's an Arquillian battle cruiser.

JAY

And we've got a dead Arquillian prince.

A COMMUNICATION STARTS COMING OVER THE SPEAKERS—a sound like a cat and mouse caught in a blender.

KAY

Message coming in.

The communication continues.

KAY (CONT'D)

Speak of the devil.

The communication continues.

JAY

They sound pissed.

ZED

(to the twins)

Translate that and step on it!

(to Kay)

Meanwhile get down to Rosenberg's store and see what you can turn up.

Kay and Jay walk away.

ZED (CONT'D)

And Kay—take a lot of fire power.

IN THE EQUIPMENT LOCKER Kay pulls out the ENORMOUS, MANY- BARRELED HAND GUN. A small, clear, canister sprouts from underneath it, malicious swirling gases visible through its walls.

JAY

I like that.

KAY

Series four de-atomizer.

Kay pulls out another weapon, the TINIEST GUN WE'VE EVER SEEN.

KAY (CONT'D)

Here. We call this the "Noisy Cricket."

JAY

You get a series four de-atomizer and I get a "Noisy Cricket?!"

(looks at the gun)

I'm afraid I'm going to break it.

Jay follows Kay out, glancing back to see the huge gun turrets on the Arquillian Battle Cruiser HUM and WHIR as they swing around into position, pointed down at the unwitting planet below.

CUT TO:

65—70 OMIT

71 INT. GEM AND JEWELRY STORE—DAY 71

SMASH! The window in the front door of Rosenberg's jewelry shop collapses in a shower of glass. EDGAR reaches in and fumbles with the locks, undoing them one by one. He gets them all and steps inside. Out the window behind him, we can see his Orkin van, double parked in the street in front.

All the gems and jewels are under glass counters. Edgar starts SMASHING the glass, grabbing great handfuls of jewels and tossing them aside.

Outside, a New York City tow truck pulls up to the front of the Orkin van and starts to hitch up.

Edgar, in his rage, starts to smash anything breakable, even the framed pictures on the walls. He stops at one particular picture, staring intently at it. It's a glamor shot of Rosenberg's cat, provocatively posed on a satin pillow. There are a half dozen more pictures of the cat, some posed with Rosenberg, some by itself. This animal was important to Rosenberg.

From outside, the ROAR of an engine distracts Edgar. He turns around, in time to see the Orkin van lurch as the tow lifts its front wheels off the ground.

72 EXT. GEM AND JEWELRY STORE—DAY 72

EDGAR rushes outside as the tow truck DRIVER gets the van up on the hoist.

EDGAR

That's my truck!

DRIVER

And make sure you tell them that at the impound.

Edgar reaches into the front seat of the van and pulls out his twelve gauge. He points it at the tow truck Driver. The tow truck driver looks at him with disdain, and pulling back his shirt reveals a mean-looking gun.

DRIVER (CONT'D)

I got worse.

He keeps hitching up the van. Two pedestrians walk past the dispute, very fast, ignoring the debate, headed right for the shop. We go with them, and realize that it's—

—JAY and KAY. They stop at the smashed door of

the jewelry shop and exchange a glance. Kay pulls a very menacing-looking weapon, nods, and they step inside.

73 INT. GEM AND JEWELRY STORE—DAY 73

They look around and see the recent demolition caused by Edgar. Jay furrows his brow.

JAY

Who robs a jewelry store and leaves the jewels?

KAY

Someone who's not looking for jewels.

Jay moves behind the counter. On the floor is an ornate, empty bowl and a bag of cat food, next to a scrumptious pillow. There are several PHOTOS OF A CAT on the wall.

There is also a pile of BEJEWELED CAT COLLARS. Jay picks up one of the COLLARS, inspects it closely, shaking his head.

JAY

This guy had a serious crush on his cat.

Jay's attention is broken by something through the window. Outside, lumbering straight for the store, is EDGAR.

Jay thinks for a moment—where does he know that face?

Suddenly, Edgar raises his arms, pointing both the farmer's rifle and the driver's shotgun. Before Edgar can shoot, Jay YELLS...

JAY

Kay! GET DOWN!

And then Jay FIRES, shattering the storefront window, and BLOWING UP A CAR on the street. The blast hurls him up and back a good ten feet, SLAMMING him into the wall with tremendous force. Edgar turns and rushes away down the street as Jay picks himself up.

JAY

The bug in the Edgar suit! The ugly redneck from the picture! That's him!

Jay leaps through the broken storefront window and after Edgar.

KAY

(picking himself up)

Damn it.

Kay runs out after Jay.

74 EXT. GEM AND JEWELRY STORE—DAY 74

Edgar doesn't bother sticking around to continue his fight. He jumps behind the wheel of the tow truck, starts it up, and hits the gas. The engine ROARS.

Jay sprints after him, FIRING his noisy cricket. He is thrown back into some pedestrians, while his SHOT...

Hits the rigging between the Orkin Van and the town truck, separating the two. Jay pulls himself up and sprints after the tow truck, but it accelerates too quickly.

Edgar is just about to turn the corner when Jay leaps onto a parked CAR to try and get some height. As Jay prepares to shoot, EDGAR DISAPPEARS AROUND THE CORNER, and a HUGH TRUCK backs into his line of fire.

JAY FIRES, the TRUCK EXPLODES and Jay flies BACKWARDS, hurtling through the air and CRASHING through the window of a car, his rear end right in the woman driver's face.

When Jay looks up, Kay is standing before him. He yanks Jay out of the car.

KAY

We don not discharge our weapons in view of the public.

JAY

Can we drop the cover-up bullshit?! There's an Alien Battle Cruiser that's gonna blow-up the world if we don't...

KAY

There's *always* an Alien Battle Cruiser...or a Korlian Death Ray, or...an intergalactic plague about to wipe out life on this planet, and the only thing that lets people get on with their hopeful little lives is that *they don't know about it.*

Kay gestures to a group of ONLOOKERS, drawn by the curious blasts from the store. There's smoking rubble everywhere.

KAY

Don't worry about the bug. He's not leaving town. We've got his ship.

After gesturing to the back of the Orkin van, where Edgar's spaceship is neatly stowed, Kay pulls out his cell phone.

KAY

(into phone)

Zed, we're gonna need a containment crew down here at McDougal, south of Houston.

A74 INT. MIB BUILDING—HEADQUARTERS—DAY A74

Back at Men in Black Headquarters, the little lights on the world map which indicate aliens' locations are going out, one by one, about one every five or ten seconds. A WARNING BUZZER is sounding, over and over, and HUMAN STAFFERS are rushing left and right.

ZED is in his office.

ZED

Containment may be a moot point, my friend. The exodus continues. It's like the party's over and the last one to leave gets stuck with the check.

Zed looks down to the vast floor below and sees the four worm guys with suitcases walking across the floor.

ZED
You sorry little ingrates!

KAY (O.S.)
What about the Arquillians?

ZED
We've only translated a part of the message so far: "Deliver the Galaxy."

KAY (O.S.)
No, they don't want much, do they?

ZED
Oh, it gets better...They're holding us responsible.

He looks up at the screen. It reads:

MIB
DELIVER THE GALAXY.

ZED
Another contestant has entered the ring.

B74 EXT. NEW YORK STREET (OUTSIDE JEWELRY STORE) B74

As Kay puts away his phone, turns to Jay

KAY
All right, kid. The Arquillians want the galaxy, whatever the hell that means. We need help. A professional. Someone with years of experience in intergalactic politics. I just hope the little prick hasn't skipped town.

CUT TO:

75 EXT. UPTOWN NEWSSTAND—DAY 75

The tow truck SQUEALS to a halt at a curb. EDGAR gets out and walks away, fast, CURSING under his breath. He rants, livid, thinking hard. As he passes a newsstand, he

grabs the NEWS VENDOR by the collar.

EDGAR

Where do you keep your dead?

VENDOR

(thinks)

I don't have any dead.

EDGAR

Where?!

VENDOR

I don't know, the city morgue!

Edgar shoves him away roughly. But before he leaves, his eye catches a postcard display marked "LANDMARKS OF THE NEW YORK CITY AREA." Edgar stares, fascinated, but we don't see what he's looking at. He reaches out and picks up a color postcard.

He raises it to his face, thinking, then shoves it in his pocket and hurries off.

CUT TO:

76 OMIT 76

77 EXT. STREET—KEY KIOSK—DAY 77

Kay's LTD SCREECHES to a halt in front of the kiosk on Orchard Street. JAY and KAY leap out and Jay spots the VENDOR, closing up the shop. He's wearing a dirty cardigan, watch cap, and fingerless gloves, his face aquiver with ticks and mannerisms. He has a small dog in front of him.

Jay rolls his eyes as they step up to the counter.

JAY

Of course that guy's an alien. That's gotta be the worst disguise I've ever seen.

A voice answers him, but not the Vendor's.

FRANK THE PUG

You don't like it, you can kiss my furry little butt.

Jay looks down. The voice is coming from the dog. *This is* FRANK THE PUG. Kay approaches, motioning to Jay to make sure no one hears.

KAY

You busy, Frank?

FRANK THE PUG

Sorry, Kay, I can't talk right now, my ride's leaving in—

Kay grabs Frank. He yelps like, well, a dog.

KAY

Call the pound. We got a stray.

FRANK THE PUG

Hey! Get your paws off me!

PASSERBYS glare at Kay, who appears to be seriously mistreating this poor little dog. Jay tries to explain.

JAY

The, uh...dog owes my friend some money.

KAY

(to Frank)

Arquillians and bugs. What do you know?

FRANK THE PUG

I know nothing.

KAY

Not a thing?

Kay shakes Frank the Pug, trying to force an answer.

FRANK THE PUG

Stop it. Okay, okay. Rosenberg wasn't some two-bit Arquillian. He was the guardian of a galaxy. They thought he would be safe here on earth.

KAY

And the bug had other plans.

FRANK THE PUG

The galaxy is the best source for subatomic energy in the universe. If the bugs get their slimy claws on it, kiss the Arquillians goodbye.

JAY

Ask him about the belt.

KAY

(to Frank)

Rosenberg said something about a galaxy on "Orion's belt." What's he talking about, Frank?

FRANK THE PUG

Beats me.

Kay shakes Frank the Pug once more.

JAY

(to a person passing by)

They're rehearsing a ventriloquist act.

FRANK THE PUG

The galaxy is here.

KAY

Here?

JAY

The galaxy is hundreds of millions of stars and planets? How's it here?

If a dog can smirk, Frank does.

FRANK THE PUG

You humans, when're you gonna learn that size doesn't matter? Just 'cause something's important, doesn't mean it's not very, very small.

KAY

How small?

FRANK THE PUG

Tiny. Like the size of a marble. Or a jewel. Now if you'll excuse me, I need to be walked before the flight.

Kay lets go of Frank, turns to Jay, who is lost in thought.

KAY

(to Frank the Pug)

Get out of here.

(then to Jay)

The galaxy's here. It's not on Orion's belt.

Jay suddenly notices Frank the Pug bark at a cat farther down the sidewalk.

JAY

Kay...

CUT TO:

78 OMIT 78

79 INT. MORGUE—DAY 79

In the morgue, LAUREL is working at a desk when suddenly ROSENBERG'S CAT leaps up onto it from nowhere, the way cats do, landing right in the middle of the file she's studying.

Laurel jumps.

LAUREL

Boy, when you want attention—

She pets the cat. As she does, the cat's collar shines in the light. Laurel turns the name tag to face her.

CLOSE ON A PRECIOUS JEWEL, AND THE WORD "ORION."

As it is written across the collar of the cat.

LAUREL (O.S)

"Orion." That's a pretty name.

From out in the corridor, a bell rings—DING, DING.

Laurel notices something dangling from the cat's collar—a CIRCULAR ICON of a strange and beautiful metal. The center is some sort of hardened, translucent material, light green in color.

LAUREL (CONT'D)

What's this?

She peers into the jewel, and her face washes over with amazement.

80 INT. ICON—DAY 80

It's as if Laurel is sucked into another universe. Her face goes beatifically blank as she sails through a massive star-field, millions of stars, billions of green, verdant planets, all racing by her at the speed of light.

81 INT. MORGUE—DAY 81

LAUREL

Wow.

Outside, the bell DINGS again. Orion looks up, as if knowing who's out there, and not liking it. She SNARLS at the door and leaps off the desk, scurrying across the lab and disappearing under some equipment.

A81 INT./EXT. LTD—MANHATTAN—DAY A81

Jay and Kay barrel through town.

JAY

So two galaxies have been fighting for years.

And the only people who've been benefiting are a race of creatures called bugs. Then the two galaxies decide to make peace...and the bugs send this guy down to make sure the fighting never stops.

KAY

By killing the emissaries, and stealing the galaxy they've been fighting about.

JAY

And if we don't get it back before he leaves the planet...*we're* history.

KAY

We're not even history. 'Cause history implies there's someone around to remember it.

82 INT. MORGUE—CORRIDOR—DAY 82

On a counter in the morgue corridor, a gray, peeling hand BANGS on a bell on a countertop, over and over. The hand belongs to EDGAR, who is carrying his shotgun, concealing it behind one leg.

The morgue attendant, TONY, emerges from a small security cage carrying a worn paperback copy of *Atlas Shrugged* and a fly swatter.

TONY

Thank you for making sure the bell works.

Suddenly, quick as a gunfighter, Tony SNAPS the fly swatter down on a BUZZING FLY. Edgar winces.

TONY (CONT'D)
(to Edgar)

What's up, Farmer John?

EDGAR

A man came in here earlier. A dead man.

TONY

And this means what to me?

EDGAR

He was a very dear friend of mine. And I believe he had an animal with him. A gift I gave him, a pet cat that means *worlds* to me. I would like it back.

TONY

I'll need a picture ID, written proof of ownership of the cat, or *notarized* proof of kinship with—

WHACK! Tony flicks the fly swatter again, sending another bug to meet its maker. Edgar grits his teeth.

TONY (CONT'D)

—the deceased.

EDGAR

Don't—do that.

WHACK! Still another fly goes down.

TONY

Do what?

Tony looks down, to where Edgar's hands rest on the counter. Half a dozen cockroaches stream out of his sleeve.

TONY (CONT'D)

Shit!

He ducks under the counter—

—and comes up with a can of Raid. Edgar's eyes bug out.

CUT TO:

83 EXT. MORGUE—DAY 83

Kay's LTD pulls to a stop in front of the morgue and JAY and KAY jump out.

JAY

I'll handle this one, you wait outside.

KAY

What the hell for?

JAY

Because all we have to do is walk in and get a cat, it's not that hard. But if you go in, you're gonna lay your Jack Webb on her and flash your brain ray in her face and she's gonna end up with leukemia or some shit. The woman's a *doctor,* she doesn't need you erasing half her med school classes. Take me five minutes.

And he continues into the morgue, leaving Kay waiting outside.

KAY

Two minutes!

84 INT. MORGUE—DAY 84

LAUREL SLAMS into a wall on one side of the morgue, thrown there by EDGAR. He leans in, close, furious.

EDGAR

Where is the animal?!

LAUREL

I *told* you, I don't *know,* it ran under some equipment! Over there.

EDGAR

Get it!

He grabs her roughly and drags her across the morgue, toward the equipment she pointed to. As they draw close, ORION the cat bolts from underneath it, races between their legs, and leapfrogs over several small cabinets, landing on top of a very tall one with only six inches clearance between it and the ceiling. A very tough hiding place.

Edgar just starts to turn when they hear the BELL and a VOICE from the corridor outside.

JAY (O.S.)

Hello? Anybody here?

Edgar looks up at the cat's hiding place. No time to get it. The bell DINGS again.

JAY (O.S.)

Hello?

Roughly, Edgar pulls Laurel close and puts a finger to his lips—*"Shhhhhhh."*

85 INT. MORGUE—CORRIDOR—DAY 85

In the corridor, JAY looks around. No Tony, no answer to the bell. He DINGS once more, then heads into the back.

86 INT. MORGUE—DAY 86

JAY comes into the morgue. LAUREL is in there, standing right up next to an examination table, but there is no corpse on the table, just a sheet draped over it. She just stands there, in the middle of the room, staring at Jay.

JAY

Uh, hi.

LAUREL
(oddly)

Hello.

JAY
(flashes a badge)

I'm Sergeant Friday, from the Twenty-Sixth precinct. They brought a cat in here with a corpse the other day, might have said "Orion" on the cat's name tag?

LAUREL

Yes. That's right.

JAY

Right, well, the cat is, uh—the cat's a witness in a murder case and I'm going to need to take it with me.

LAUREL

I don't know where the cat is at the moment.

JAY

You don't?

LAUREL

No.

(lowers her voice to a whisper)

Maybe you could take *me* with you instead.

Jay looks at her.

JAY

Excuse me?

LAUREL

I said, maybe you could take me with you instead.

JAY

Damn, you do start fast, don't you?

LAUREL

I'd really like to go with you. Now.

Jay just looks at her, amazed at the power he seems to have over this woman. He looks over his shoulder, to make sure he has a few more seconds alone.

JAY

And, uh, why exactly is that?

Laurel rolls her eyes. She seems irritated with him, but it doesn't go with what she's saying.

LAUREL

I just *do*.

87 INT. MORGUE—CORRIDOR—DAY 87

KAY comes down the stairs and into the morgue corridor. He checks his watch, then leans against the counter and pulls out a pack of cigarettes. Waiting.

88 INT. MORGUE—DAY 88

Jay is thoroughly enjoying himself, but Laurel seems to be going crazy.

LAUREL

I have something I need to show you.

She looks down, pointedly, in the direction of her waist.

JAY

Now slow down, you don't have to hit the gas like that.

She leans in and lowers her voice.

LAUREL

You don't understand. You really need to see this.

JAY

And I will. But we gotta get something straight here—I'm gonna drive. It's not some kind of macho trip, it's just the way I'm used to doing things, okay?

89 INT. MORGUE—CORRIDOR—DAY 89

Kay pulls out a box of matches and strikes one on the side. He raises it to his cigarette, but as it draws close, the match goes out with a sharp SIZZLE.

Kay furrows his brow. Odd.

90 INT. MORGUE—DAY 90

Laurel is at the end of her rope.

LAUREL

Look, Stud, I don't know how many more times I'm going to get to tell you this. There's *something—*

She points, sharply, at the examination table directly in front of her.

LAUREL (CONT'D)

—that you have to help me with.

Jay's smile vanishes and his jaw drops as he figures it out. He starts to reach for his gun.

91 INT. MORGUE—CORRIDOR—DAY 91

Kay raises another lit match to his cigarette, but as this one gets close, a BIG GLOB OF GOO drops from the ceiling and onto the match, dousing the flame.

Kay looks up, sharply.

Above him, TONY, the counter guy, is stuck to one high corner of the ceiling by an enormous wad of viscous, dripping fluid. He's dead, a frozen look of terror on his face and the can of Raid still clutched in his hand.

From inside the morgue, Laurel SCREAMS.

92 INT. MORGUE—DAY 92

Kay races into the morgue just as the examination table EXPLODES into the air, revealing EDGAR, who was hiding beneath it.

Now everything happens at once. Jay leaps back and draws the Noisy Cricket, Kay pulls out his series four deatomizer, and Edgar holds his shotgun under Laurel's chin, using her body to shield his own.

KAY

Freeze it, Bug!

JAY

Don't shoot! Don't shoot!

LAUREL

(to Jay)

CHRIST, are you THICK!

JAY

How was I supposed to know!?!

LAUREL

What did I have to do, SING it for you!?!

JAY

Maybe if you didn't come on like a drunken prom date!

LAUREL

Oh, that's SO typical. Any time a woman shows the slightest hint of sexual independence, men just—

EDGAR

Everybody shut UP!

KAY

Let her go, Shit Eater.

EDGAR

Listen, Monkey Boy, I may have to take that kind of talk in my end of the universe, but compared to you humans, I'm the top rung on the evolutionary ladder, *so can it, all right?!*

KAY

You're breakin' my heart. Move six inches to your left and I'll solve all your problems.

ORION the cat suddenly attacks, leaping off the top of the cabinet and landing on Edgar, HISSING and scratching and clawing for all she's worth. Edgar snaps an arm up and whips her off. The cat squirms in his arm, the icon jangling. Edgar grabs the icon, holds onto it, and *flings* the cat away, across the morgue. The icon comes free, remaining in his hand.

He *drops it into his mouth* and swallows. He shoves the gun hard against Laurel's cheek.

EDGAR

That's better. Now put down your weapons. We're leaving.

Kay freezes, teeth clenched, gun still in front of him. Standoff.

EDGAR (CONT'D)

Have you ever pulled the wings off a fly?

Edgar cranks one of Laurel's arms behind her back, hard, and she CRIES OUT in pain.

EDGAR (CONT'D)

Would you care to see the fly get even?

KAY

How far you think you'll get without your ship? If that's what you call that hunk of space crap we've got back at our office.

EDGAR

Put the weapons down!

KAY

Never gonna happen, Insect.

Edgar backs away with Laurel, further into the morgue,

toward a glass window that looks out at the base of an air shaft. Jay and Kay advance, slowly, cornering him.

JAY

It's okay, Laurel!

LAUREL

HOW is it okay?!

JAY

I mean it's *going* to be okay!

EDGAR

Don't bet on it, meat sack.

And with that he turns, leaps—

—and CRASHES right through the window, into the air shaft.

93 EXT. MORGUE (SIDE STREET)—DUSK 93

EDGAR, still clutching LAUREL, EXPLODES up over a railing.

Nobody looks twice as Edgar, dragging Laurel (with his arm over her mouth), races toward the nearby busy Manhattan Street.

94 INT. MORGUE—AIR SHAFT—DUSK 94

Jay and Kay duck into the air shaft and look up—too far to climb, and the walls are smooth anyway.

KAY

Damn it!

They turn and run out of the morgue.

A94 EXT. THE NEARBY BUSY MANHATTAN STREET—DUSK A94

EDGAR, with LAUREL, RUNS *right in front of a CAB,* which screeches to a halt inches from them. The CABBIE sticks his head out and YELLS something in an unknown language. And KEEPS yelling as—

Edgar reaches through the passenger side and pulls the Cabbie out the door (cigarette and wooden seat-beads and all).

The Cab Driver is still yelling as Edgar leaps in, pushing Laurel in before him, leaving her behind the wheel.

He removes a POSTCARD—the one he took from the display on the newsstand.

EDGAR

Take me *here.*

LAUREL

What???

Edgar just cranks the car into gear—opening his mouth and swallowing the icon—and in so doing revealing a TRIPLE ROW OF SERRATED BUG-TEETH, *he SLAMS HIS FOOT on the gas pedal.*

Laurel's head snaps back as the car rocks forward. She has no choice, but to grab the wheel and start steering as—

The car screeches out into traffic, swerving wildly as Laurel is forced to make a 90-degree turn. The car fishtails wildly, swiping an oncoming car as it straightens and heads into the traffic.

The furious Cab Driver runs off after it, still yelling as he disappears around the corner

A second later, KAY and JAY rush out into the street. The cab is nowhere to be seen. Jay runs into the street, noticing the wooden beads, the ripped pine-scented green deodorizer, and the still-burning cigarette.

JAY

They're in a cab.

And Jay starts running down the street, where DOZENS of cabs are waiting at the intersection. He's running from cab to cab, pounding on windows, scaring the living shit out of people—

JAY

Hey! Laurel!? Hey!

—but Laurel and Edgar are nowhere to be found. Up ahead the light turns green and the tide of taxis wash away, leaving Jay on the street. He turns as a car screeches up behind him, its headlights shining in his eyes. As it gets closer, Jay sees it's Kay in the LTD.

KAY

Stop wasting time. He's not getting off the planet in a cab.

95 OMITTED 95

CUT TO:

96 INT. MIB BUILDING—HEADQUARTERS—NIGHT 96

Jay and Kay rush in from the door under the World's Fair mural, and head toward the main display screen; all around them, the MIB staffers are in frenetic activity in response to the threat from above.

KAY

(to tech at a desk)

Come with me. Put up a bio-net all the way around Manhattan; if it's not human, it's not leaving the island.

KAY (CONT'D)

What've we got from our friends upstairs?

ZED

Same thing: "Deliver the galaxy."

KAY

Yeah, well the bug's got the galaxy, but we've got his ship. He's got to be looking for a way out.

Just then, a loud ALARM wails.

AT THE MAIN VIEWING SCREEN, A GREEN LINE shoots out from the Arquillian ship, striking a region of planet earth.

97 OMIT 97

98 OMIT 98

99 OMIT 99

100 INT. MIB BUILDING—HEADQUARTERS—NIGHT 100

—headquarters, where every bell, whistle and light imaginable is going off.

JAY

WHAT THE HELL ARE THEY SHOOTING AT *US* FOR?!

ZED

Arquillian battle rules, kid. First we get an ultimatum, then a warning shot, then we have a galactic standard week to respond.

JAY

A galactic standard week? How the hell long is that?

KAY

One hour.

JAY

One hour?

Viewing the screen, it now reads:

MIB
DELIVER THE GALAXY
OR THE EARTH WILL BE DESTROYED...
SORRY

ZED

To keep the bugs from getting it, the Arquillians will destroy the galaxy and whatever planet it's on.

JAY

You're talking about US!

ZED

Sucks, doesn't it?

KAY

Pull up the locations of all land-based interstellar vehicles.

ZED

They're all gone. Frank the Pug took the last ship on the planet.

As Kay and Zed watch as the machine scrolls through the

data, Jay walks back towards the center of the room, deep in thought. Over him we hear:

KAY

Atlantic City?

ZED

Gone.

KAY

That landfill on the Jersey Shore?

ZED

Gone.

JAY

Uh, gentlemen.

KAY

Epcot?

ZED

Gone.

KAY

Miami Beach?

ZED

Gone.

JAY

Fellas.

KAY

Hartford?

ZED

Gone, thank God.

JAY

Hey. *Old guys.*

Kay and Zed both look up at once, scowling.

JAY (CONT'D)

Do *those* still work?

They follow his gaze, up, over the computer terminals. There, on the wall in front of them, where it has loomed for the entire movie, is the enormous mural of the 1964 World's Fair grounds. Most prominent in the mural are two tall towers that rise dramatically from the ground, topped by—

—the two flying saucers from the very first alien contact. As they stand there, wide-eyed, staring at it, we—

DISSOLVE TO:

101 EXT. WORLD'S FAIR—NIGHT 101

—the real-live twin towers on the actual fairgrounds in Flushing Meadows. A taxi SCREECHES to a halt at the edge of a fence a hundred yards away. EDGAR shoves LAUREL out through the driver's door and follows behind her, still holding his weapon on her.

EDGAR

You're coming with me.

LAUREL

What?! *Why?!*

EDGAR

It's a long trip. I'll need a snack.

And he shoves her ahead of him, off in the direction of the space ships.

Behind him, abandoned on the front seat of the cab, we finally see the front of the postcard he's been carrying around. "FLUSHING MEADOWS, SITE OF THE 1964 WORLD'S FAIR," it says, with a distinctive photograph of the spaceships.

So *that's* how he knew.

CUT TO:

102 EXT. COLUMBUS CIRCLE—NIGHT 102

Nighttime now, and the city hums along, just another Thursday night. The clock in Columbus Circle says it's 7:45.

103 EXT. SIXTH AVENUE—NIGHT 103

TVs in the window of an appliance store show a rerun of "Cheers." PEOPLE laugh.

104 EXT. TIMES SQUARE—NIGHT 104

The news ticker in Times Square announces the latest shattering news:

RAIN LIKELY—TEMPS DROP TO 60'S

EARTHLINGS pass left and right, blissfully unaware of their impending doom.

CUT TO:

105 EXT. MIB BUILDING—NIGHT 105

KAY and JAY leap into Kay's LTD and SLAM the doors. Kay jams the key in the ignition, the car ROARS to life, and he turns to Jay.

KAY

Whaddya say we bag us some bug?

He hits the gas and the car ROCKETS away from the curb.

106 EXT. CITY STREETS—NIGHT 106

The LTD tears through the city.

107 INT. MIB LTD—TRAVELING—NIGHT 107

Kay turns sharply to the right, SMACKING Jay around. Looking up ahead, he sees the entrance to the midtown tunnel.

JAY

You're taking the tunnel?!

KAY

You know a better way to Queens?

JAY

It's usually jammed?!

108 EXT. MIDTOWN TUNNEL—NIGHT 108

The LTD races through the tunnel at top speed. It's clear driving for a few seconds, but then they round a bend —

—*and there's a traffic jam up ahead.*

109 INT. MIB LTD—TRAVELING—NIGHT 109

Kay approaches the line of cars at top speed, with no intention of slowing down. Jay, terrified, holds on for dear life.

JAY

I told you!

KAY

Jay. The button?

JAY

Yeah?!

KAY

Push the button, Jay.

A LIGHTED PANEL rotates into place between the two front seats, and that red button flashes underneath its plastic shield again. Jay flips back the plastic cover and JAMS his finger down on the red flashing button.

KAY (CONT'D)

And you *may* want to throw on a seat belt.

110 EXT. MIDTOWN TUNNEL—MIB LTD—NIGHT 110

As the LTD rockets toward the traffic jam up ahead, it begins to evolve, its shape actually *changing*. The sides and back extend as some sort of endoskeleton pushes the "normal" panels out. It becomes a larger, wirier machine, held together by an elaborate series of mechanical muscles and metallic tendons.

Kay's car hurtles toward certain death in the traffic jam, but at the last possible moment it swerves off to the side, a SUCKING SOUND coming from underneath it.

Instead of banging *off* the wall of the tunnel, the LTD actually *clings* to it. It swerves up, onto the wall and hangs there, racing by the traffic below.

It keeps going, turning all the way over and driving upside down, wheels clinging to the roof of the tunnel.

111 INT. MIB LTD—TRAVELING—NIGHT 111

Jay falls from his seat with a CLUNK, onto the upside-down ceiling of the car. Balled up on the back of his neck, he peers out the window as they tear through the tunnel, ZOOMING over the bottlenecked traffic underneath.

As they race through the tunnel, they have a minute to kill.

KAY

Mind if I smoke?

JAY

What?!?

KAY

In the car, I mean.

JAY

I don't care!!

KAY

Hey, just a common courtesy. It bothers some people if you smoke in a car.

He lights a cigarette and blows the smoke out leisurely, one hand on the wheel, just waiting out the tunnel. Jay gives up struggling to right himself and closes his eyes, suffering through this.

112 EXT. MIB LTD—TRAVELING—NIGHT 112

From outside the car, we watch it rocket along on the roof of the tunnel. We can hear KAY'S VOICE as he goes on. And on.

KAY

Yeah, it's harder and harder to smoke anywhere these days. Hell, I suppose I should quit. I've tried. Never took, though. I'm beginning to think I lack self-control.

And they disappear out the other end of the tunnel—

113 INT. MIB LTD—TRAVELING—NIGHT 113

—and flip over, BANGING back down onto the road on the other side. Jay falls off the ceiling and SLAMS into his seat.

KAY

Well, back to work.

He flips his cigarette out the window and cranks the wheel to the left.

114 EXT. MIDTOWN TUNNEL—TOLL BOOTH—NIGHT 114

Approaching a toll booth, the LTD shoots across nine lanes of traffic and through the only open booth, SHATTERING the gate. Traveling at about two hundred miles an hour, Kay nonchalantly flips a token out the window—

—and it CHINKS in the basket as their taillights disappear.

CUT TO:

115 EXT. WORLD'S FAIR—LANDING TOWER—NIGHT 115

EDGAR climbs the outside of the landing tower of one of the space ships, pushing LAUREL up ahead of him, headed for the saucer at the top.

LAUREL

Come on, let me go, you don't want to eat me. I'm a very important person on my planet. Like a queen. A goddess, even. There are those who worship me, yes. I'm not trying to impress you with this, I'm just letting you know. It could start a war.

EDGAR

Good. War means food for my family, all seventy-eight million of them. That's a lot of mouths to feed, your highness.

LAUREL

You're a wonderful dad.

And with that she KICKS him squarely in the face. He reels, momentarily losing his grip on her. She takes advantage of the moment and FLINGS HERSELF out, into the air.

Edgar flails, but she is beyond his reach. She falls, tumbling through the air—

—and lands in the branches of a tree. She hits hard, the branches rattling, and reaches out and hangs on for dear life, high above the ground.

Above, Edgar just keeps climbing.

116 EXT. WORLD'S FAIR—NIGHT 116

Over at the fence, the LTD comes to a looooong, skidding stop at the fairgrounds.

AT THE TRUNK, JAY and KAY flip open the trunk and scarf up whatever weapons look most dangerous. Kay grabs a black box, UNSNAPS a row of latches, and opens it, revealing—

—*the most wicked-looking shotgun on the planet.*

Three feet long, triple-barreled, over and under and under, plus a pump action reloader on top of a storage clip for a dozen more shells. The shells themselves are solid, glistening like polished steel. Kay loads up the clip.

JAY

You know how to work that?

Kay pumps it once, with extreme confidence.

KAY

No idea whatsoever.

He SLAMS the trunk, revealing the flying saucers sitting atop their columns in the distance.

KAY (CONT'D)

Let's bag us some bug.

As if on cue, one of the saucers begins to HUM. Then it starts to spin, faster and faster. The ship begins to rise.

JAY

Oh, shit.

117 EXT. WORLD'S FAIR—TREE—NIGHT 117

Laurel sits in her tree, watching with amazement.

118 EXT. SHEA STADIUM—NIGHT 118

At Shea Stadium, a Mets game is in progress. Behind the home plate side, the flying saucer silently rises up in the night sky, plainly visible.

But at that very moment, the batter CRACKS into a fastball, hard. The crowd rises to its feet, SHOUTING, staring out at center field, where the ball is headed.

All eyes in the house are on the Mets' CENTER FIELDER, except for *his* eyes, which are on the flying saucer behind home plate. His eyes widen, his jaw drops—

—and the catchable ball sails over his head, THUDDING into the wall behind him. The crowd BOOS viciously.

119 EXT. WORLD'S FAIR—NIGHT 119

Kay raises the weapon he took from the trunk; looks over at Jay.

KAY

Set it to pulsar level five, sub-sonic implosion factor—

JAY

What?

KAY

Press the little green button, on three.

Jay raises his weapon; they press their green buttons.

KAY (CONT'D)

One...two...

They pull their triggers.

For a moment, nothing happens, as if it were a misfire. But then, there is a VACUUM WHUMP, like all the air in the immediate area being sucked into a space the size of a dime, and a tremendous *shock wave* rolls out from the barrel of the guns.

Jay and Kay are sucked to the ground by the bizarre force, THUDDING to their stomachs like magnets to a refrigerator.

120 OMIT 120

A120 EXT. WORLD'S FAIR—NIGHT A120

The shock waves wrinkle across the open space between them and the ship, then it *HITS* the ship—

—and it too is sucked back down. Hurtling back toward them.

B120 EXT. LAUREL'S TREE—NIGHT B120

She flinches as the flying saucer shoots overhead.

121 EXT. WORLD'S FAIR—NIGHT 121

The saucer CRASHES through the Unisphere, an enormous steel globe, and THUDS to the earth, CRASHING through brush, dirt and rock...

Jay and Kay come to their feet...

In front of them, the dust clears...Trees uprooted, stones and dirt thrown everywhere...a dumpster has been cast to their left...

And the saucer is there, embedded in the earth, tipped off-kilter in a mound of debris...

A hatch comes up...revealing Edgar, walking slowly toward them, with contained fury.

EDGAR

You don't get it. I've won. It's over.

KAY

You are under arrest for violating number 4-1-53 of the Tycho accord. Please hand over any galaxy you might be carrying.

EDGAR

You milk-suckers! You don't matter! In a few seconds you won't even *be* matter!

KAY

Move away from the vehicle and put your hands on your head.

He pumps the gun for emphasis.

EDGAR

Put my hands on my head?

Edgar stares at him. Then flexes his arms, still encased in flesh. His giant pincers RIP free of the rotting skin.

He extends both pincers to the sides, and, my God, his reach must be twelve feet across.

Now the skin and clothes on Edgar's legs begins to CRACK and SHRED. They BURST APART, revealing two hideous, doubled-over insect legs. The bug raises himself aloft on his legs.

He sucks in a deep breath of air, and now the rest of the Edgar suit goes the way of the arms and legs. The torso EXPLODES in great rendering of cloth and skin, and finally

Edgar's head simply BURSTS apart, SPATTERING against the walls. Edgar now reveals himself as he really is: a hairy, bug-like exoskeleton, a scaly tail with a long stinger, a head like a cobra with elliptical eyes and a small nose, and two horse-like feet with three toes each.

He raises his pincers in the air, resting them on his

head. The GALAXY hangs on a chain around his neck.

BUG

Like this?

Kay and Jay pump their guns and aim at the Bug.

Suddenly the Bug SPITS. And a HUGE, SLIMY WAD OF GOO shoots from him and engulfs both shotguns. The Bug snorts it back, tearing them from Jay and Kay's grasp, then swallowing them.

Jay and Kay have only a second to react before—

The Bug SWIPES at them with the back of his clawed hand, like someone brushing aside a gnat—and SENDS THEM FLYING FIFTEEN FEET IN THE AIR.

A121 EXT. LAUREL'S TREE—NIGHT A121

She flinches as she sees them hit the ground. She starts to climb the tree.

B121 EXT. WORLD'S FAIR—NIGHT B121

Jay and Kay hit the ground with loud grunts.

JAY

That did not go at *all* like I had planned.

They look up to see the Bug moving for the second

tower—and the second flying saucer. Kay gets to his feet.

KAY

This guy's really starting to bug me.

Kay starts walking after the Bug.

KAY

Whatever happens, Jay, don't let him get on that ship.

JAY

Where are you going?

KAY

Getting my gun back.

JAY

What!?

Kay steps forward and yells at the departing Bug.

KAY (CONT'D)

Hey, Bug!

The Bug just keeps moving toward the ladder.

KAY (CONT'D)

I'm talking to you, Bug! You know how many of your kind I've swatted with a newspaper?

The Bug turns toward Kay. Kay steps up to him, the small human facing off against the giant alien bug.

122 — 123 OMITTED

124 EXT. LAUREL'S TREE—NIGHT 124

She quietly makes it to the ground—hurries off to the darkness of the woods.

125 EXT. WORLD'S FAIR—ON KAY AND THE BUG—NIGHT 125

Kay has himself in the Bug's face, its dripping fangs inches from Kay's face.

KAY

You're just a smear on the sports page to me, you slimy, gut-sucking, intestinal parasite! Eat me!

The Bug reacts—cranks open its massive jaws with a deafening HISS, lunges forward, and *sucks Kay into his mouth.*

The Bug straightens up to its full height and throws his head back. Kay slides down the Bug's throat, bending it sideways as he kicks and SCREAMS his way down into its abdomen.

JAY looks on, in stunned horror...

AS THE BUG TURNS TO JAY AND STRETCHES TO ITS FULL HEIGHT and lets loose a HIDEOUS SCREAMING HOWL OF TRIUMPH.

126 EXT. WOODS—NIGHT 126

Laurel is still watching.

127 EXT. WORLD'S FAIR—ON JAY AND THE BUG—NIGHT 127

Jay watches as the Bug continues its HOWL OF TRIUMPH...He feels totally defeated. But...

He can hardly believe his eyes as he looks down at the Bug's stomach...

CLOSE ON BUG'S STOMACH. Through the leathery pouch of the Bug's stomach, we can just make out the distended outline of the two atomizers...and just a few inches from it, a HUMAN HAND is reaching toward the gun...KAY!

A127 INT. BUG—NIGHT A127

Kay, swimming in the Bug's intestinal fluid, tries to make his way to the gun, Holding his breath. Eyes stinging.

B127 EXT. WORLD'S FAIR—NIGHT B127

Jay knows what he has to do. He picks up a good-sized chunk of concrete dislodged by the crashing saucer and hurls it at the Bug.

JAY

Hey! Come over here and try that!

The concrete THUNKS off the Bug's shell—he doesn't seem to notice; just keeps moving.

Jay picks up a twisted metal pole and runs at the Bug.

JAY

Stop right there, or I'll start wailing on your waxy, pointed ass!

Jay starts pounding on the Bug with the metal pole.

C127 INT. BUG—NIGHT C127

Kay *almost* has his fingers around the stock of the gun—The POUNDING on the outside distracts him and he turns—the gun shifts away.

D127 EXT. WORLD'S FAIR—NIGHT D127

The Bug grabs the metal pole and yanks it out of Jay's hands. He swings at Jay—Jay dodges the blow and falls to the grass.

The Bug *slices* down with razor-sharp claws at Jay—

—Jay rolls out of the way, just as the mean-looking claws dig into the grass.

Jay rolls *right underneath* the Bug's legs. His hand falls on something in the grass—another piece of debris, a *sharp metal spike,* gleaming like a dagger. He grabs the metal spike and looks up at the Bug's apparently vulnerable underbelly, right above him.

He grabs the spike with both hands and is about to *thrust the spike up,* into the Bug's gut, when;

The Bug bends its head down between its legs.

BUG'S POV of Jay there, upside-down from this perspective, lurking between the Bug's legs.

E127 EXT. WORLD'S FAIR—NIGHT E127

The Bug opens its jaws and SNAPS at Jay—who propels himself backward out of harm's way.

The Bug starts climbing the tower. Jay howls in frustration.

JAY

What are you, afraid of me? Come on! Stand and fight like an arthropod!

In frustration, Jay screams and throws himself on the Bug, hanging onto its back, trying to drag it down.

JAY (CONT'D)

You want a piece of this, huh?! Maybe you're a badass in your hive, but this is New York City. You're just another tourist here!

The Bug flicks him off with his tail—sending him SAILING twenty feet through the air.

Jay CRASHES into the dumpster, landing on a heap in front of the garbage.

But, scratched and beat-up, Jay still doesn't quit—he stands to yell at the Bug, extending his arm at the creature.

JAY

You're messing with the wrong species, Bug—

He notices something on his arm...a *cockroach* running down his sleeve. He flicks it off...

Looks down at the ground...sees another roach...looks over to the dumpster behind him...there are more of them...a whole mob, in fact...fifty or sixty of the critters, climbing out of a rusted hole in the dumpster...

Jay has one last desperate idea...He kicks at the dumpster—part of the side is rusted paper thin and it kicks apart and crumbles to pieces.

TENS OF THOUSANDS OF ROACHES pouring forth from the dumpster, crawling like a black glittering river, away from the garbage...

Jay leaps to his feet and moves to the glistening mob of insects...

JAY

Hey, Bug!

CLOSE ON JAY'S FOOT as he steps on the roach.

CRUNCH.

ON THE BUG as he *flinches* on the ladder—he hates that sound.

ON JAY. He smiles.

JAY (CONT'D)

If I'm not mistaken, that was a cousin of yours.

He knows he's getting to him. He steps toward the Bug—moving his foot over another roach.

CRUNCH! He crushes another one.

JAY (CONT'D)

Whoa! That had to hurt. And, what d'you know, here's your old Uncle Bob!

He steps forward again—CRUNCH!

ON THE BUG. He turns around, anger burning in his eyes.

F127 INT. BUG—NIGHT F127

Kay's hand reaches closer and closer to the gun...

128 OMITTED 128

129 EXT. WORLD'S FAIR—ON JAY—NIGHT 129

Jay keeps moving toward the Bug, finding new roaches to tread on—holds his foot over another one.

JAY

What's that? Can you hear what he's saying? 'Help me! Help me!'

CRUNCH. [ON] THE BUG as he starts climbing down the tower and moving toward Jay.

ON JAY. They are moving toward each other in a show down—Jay moves on, poising his foot over another roach.

JAY

Ooh! There's a pretty one. That one looks kinda familiar, don't you think? I know who that is!

The Bug is right over Jay now, jaws dripping ready to gobble him up.

BUG

Don't do that!

Jay stares right back at the Bug. Inside, he sees Kay's hand, closing around the trigger of the shotgun. He brings it around, pointing up, straight at the Bug's head.

JAY

That's your Momma!

He moves to CRUNCH the roach—The Bug moves to chomp Jay—Jay stares up at him, unflinching...

JAY (CONT'D)

Didn't she ever teach you not to bite off more than you can chew?

and at that very moment...

Kay BLASTS a hole right in the middle of the Bug's midsection. The front of the Bug's thorax EXPLODES in a shower of bug juice all over Jay.

The Bug flies into two pieces—the butt end sailing one way; the head flying behind Jay.

Kay falls out of the Bug, in a mess of goo, gasping for breath, dropping the atomizer from his slippery fingers.

The other gun sails off into the darkness.

The ICON drops to the ground, rolls over to Jay's feet, and CLATTERS to rest like a silver dollar on a barroom floor.

He calmly bends down and picks it up. Jay is pissed and starts in on Kay.

JAY

You son of a—

Kay holds up a finger in a 'wait a minute' gesture—pulls out his pocket phone and hits a number.

KAY

Zed. Get a message to the Arquillians. We have the galaxy.

130—134 OMITTED

A134 INT. MIB HEADQUARTERS—NIGHT A134

Zed is standing at the console, a smile on his face. He glances over at the console that displays alien arrivals and departures on the earth. *The red lights are coming back on.*

ZED

I think the word's already out. Our friends are coming back.

(then)

Got an authorized landing at Times Square. You and Jay check it out on the way back...And pick me up one of those soft pretzels, while you're at it. Extra salt. I feel like celebrating.

B134 EXT. WORLD'S FAIR—NIGHT B134

Kay flips the phone closed.

KAY

You were saying?

JAY

Getting eaten!? That was your plan!?

KAY

(shrugs)

Worked.

As they argue, behind them, unseen, THE FRONT HALF OF THE BUG RAISES ITSELF UP on its forearms, eyes gleaming with hate, jaws dripping—ready to lower itself onto Kay and Jay.

JAY

After I got the shit beat out of me!

KAY

And I almost got digested. It goes with the job.

JAY

You coulda told me what you were doing.

KAY

There wasn't time, sport!

HISSS! The Bug attacks, swinging its head down on them. They turn to see it, and just before the jaws snap down on their heads...

BOOM! The Bug's head explodes into a million bits. Bug juice showers down everywhere, bucketsful of goo drenching Kay and Jay even further.

They turn to see...

LAUREL standing behind the dead Bug, the other atomizer in her hands, the barrel smoking, the weapon and Laurel dripping the Bug innards.

LAUREL

Interesting job you guys got.

ON THE SKY. Bits of Bug juice still flying through the air.

C134 INT. A CAR ON THE ADJOINING FREEWAY—NIGHT C134

The driver sees something tumbling toward the windshield. He winces.

—AND THE BUG'S REMAINS SPLAT AGAINST THE WINDSHIELD.

The driver grimaces at the mess.

DRIVER

Damn bugs.

He reaches down and hits a button. Wiper fluid squirts onto the windshield and the wipers spread the bug goo everywhere.

CUT TO:

135 EXT. MIB BUILDING—NIGHT 135

Kay's LTD is parked outside Men in Black headquarters. LAUREL leans her back against the car. We see JAY and KAY walking away in the distance.

JAY

Look, I know we got rules, but she did just bust the Bug for us. And so maybe you don't have to flashy thing her.

Kay pulls out the neuralyzer.

JAY

Who's she gonna tell, anyway? She only hangs out with dead people.

KAY

Not her. Me.

(looking up at the sky)

They're beautiful, aren't they? The stars. I never just look anymore and they're beautiful.

JAY

Kay, you're scaring your partner.

KAY

I haven't been training a partner—I've been training a replacement.

JAY

Oh no, I can't do this job by myself.

LAUREL

(walking towards them)

Hey, guys, we're nowhere near my apartment. We're not even on the right island.

KAY

Maybe you won't have to.

Kay starts dialing back the neuralyzer.

KAY

Days. Months. Years. Always face it forwards.

He hands the neuralyzer to Jay. Taps his pocket. Indicates for him to put his glasses on. Jay resists.

KAY

I've just been down the gullet of an interstellar cockroach. That's one of a hundred memories I don't want.

Jay takes the neuralizer. Slips on his glasses.

KAY

See you around, sport.

Jay raises the neuralyzer. With a brilliant FLASH, the screen turns white.

JAY

No, you won't.

CUT TO:

136 EXT. NEWSSTAND—DAY 136

CLOSE ON various tabloid headlines as a hand flicks through them. Here's one:

Mets' Centerfielder Says:
"UFO MADE ME MISS HOME RUN BALL!"

And here's another one:

DETROIT HAS CAR THAT DEFIES GRAVITY!
Secret Tests in N.Y.'s Tunnel

And a third:

MAN AWAKENS FROM 30-YEAR COMA
Returns to Girl He Left Behind

A large photograph shows a smiling KAY, arm-in-arm with ELIZABETH RESTON, his long-lost fiancee, in her back yard in Tempe, Arizona.

She holds a large bouquet of flowers, the same kind he brought but never gave her thirty years ago.

JAY, who's reading the paper, smiles.

AT THE CURB, Jay hurries back to the LTD with the newspapers. ELLE, (formerly Laurel), is waiting, leaning against the hood. Tailored black suit. Black shoes. Short-cropped hair. The look never looked better.

ELLE

Zed called. The High Consulate of Regent-9 emissary wants floor seats to the Knicks–Bulls game.

JAY

I'll talk to Dennis Rodman, it's his damn planet.

ELLE

Let's roll.

Both car doors SLAM, Jay drops it in gear, and the LTD BLASTS away from the curb.

137 EXT. NEW YORK CITY BLOCK—DAY 137

The LTD is just one of many cars in a jam-packed Manhattan city block.

138 FROM UP IN THE CLOUDS 138

Manhattan itself is just part of a much larger urban and suburban sprawl.

139 FROM THE STRATOSPHERE 139

The east coast of the United States is just part of a much larger land mass.

140 FROM THE EOSPHERE 140

North America is just a small portion of the planet Earth.

141 FROM SPACE 141

Earth is just a tiny ball in our solar system.

142 FROM THE MIDDLE OF THE MILKY WAY 142

Our solar system is just a few blips of light in a vast star field.

143 FROM OUTSIDE OUR GALAXY 143

The Milky Way is just a creamy spiral amid innumerable other creamy spirals.

144 FROM THE OUTER REACHES OF THE UNIVERSE 144

There seems to be an edge to what we see, a curved border that seems to close in on things around the perimeters, until everything that exists seems to be contained in one tiny ball—

—which is actually a marble resting on a strange-looking patch of red dirt.

An ALIEN HAND reaches down and flicks the marble, sending it skittering and bouncing across the dirt, where it CLICKS into a dozen other big blue balls just like it.

FADE OUT.

COLUMBIA PICTURES Presents

An AMBLIN ENTERTAINMENT Production

In association with MacDONALD/PARKES Productions

A BARRY SONNENFELD Film

Starring

TOMMY LEE JONES WILL SMITH

MIB
MEN IN BLACK™

LINDA FIORENTINO

VINCENT D'ONOFRIO

RIP TORN

Associate Producer STEVEN R. MOLEN

Alien Make-up Effects by RICK BAKER

Special Animation and Visual Effects by
INDUSTRIAL LIGHT & MAGIC

Music by DANNY ELFMAN

Film Editor JIM MILLER

Production Designer BO WELCH

Director of Photography DON PETERMAN, ASC

Co-producer GRAHAM PLACE

Executive Producer STEVEN SPIELBERG

Based on the Malibu Comic by LOWELL CUNNINGHAM

Screen Story and Screenplay by ED SOLOMON

Produced by WALTER F. PARKES and LAURIE MacDONALD

Directed by BARRY SONNENFELD

ABOUT THE AUTHORS

Barry Sonnenfeld

Men in Black director Sonnenfeld most recently directed the hit comedy *Get Shorty,* which received a Golden Globe nomination for Best Comedy and a Golden Globe Award for John Travolta. Sonnenfeld earned acclaim for his innovative work on the box-office success *The Addams Family,* which was his feature film directorial debut. He later directed the sequel *Addams Family Values*. Both films starred the late Raul Julia, Angelica Huston, Christina Ricci, and Christopher Lloyd, and created a new generation of fans for the uniquely macabre family created by cartoonist Charles Addams and first portrayed in the classic television series. Sonnenfeld also directed the comedy *For Love or Money,* starring Michael J. Fox.

Prior to becoming a director, Sonnenfeld was an award-winning cinematographer. He collaborated with Danny DeVito on *Throw Momma From the Train*. He also lensed *When Harry Met Sally* and *Misery* for director Rob Reiner, and *Big* for Penny Marshall. His additional film credits as a director of photography include the Coen brothers' *Blood Simple, Raising Arizona,* and *Miller's Crossing,* and Phil Joanu's *Three O'Clock High*.

In addition to his film work, Sonnenfeld has directed numerous commercials, two of which have won Clio Awards: "Dog" for Nike; and "Tennis Balls" for Reebok. He is also the director of the inventive Duracell "Putterman Family" commercials.

For the small screen, Sonnenfeld was honored with an Emmy Award for his cinematography on the 1985 ABC special *Out of Step*.

Ed Solomon

Men in Black's screenwriter also co-wrote the screenplays for *Bill and Ted's Excellent Adventure* and *Bill and Ted's Bogus Journey,* and wrote the screenplay for *Leaving Normal*.

For television, he was one of the original writers for *It's Garry Shandling's Show,* and continued with the show for three years. Currently Solomon and Shandling are collaborating on a film for Columbia Pictures, *What Planet Are You From?,* and Solomon is scripting *X-Men* for director Bryan Singer and Twentieth-Century Fox. He is also directing his first indie feature, *Levity.*

Solomon, his wife, Cynthia, and their son, Evan (born in March 1997), live in Santa Monica.

Laurie MacDonald

MacDonald, producer of *Men in Black* with Walter F. Parkes, began her career as a news and documentary producer for the NBC affiliate in San Francisco, eventually producing *SFO,* a nightly news and entertainment magazine show in the Bay Area. In 1984, she moved to Los Angeles and became a creative executive at Columbia Pictures, and was promoted to vice president of production one year later.

MacDonald first collaborated with Parkes in 1988 on *True Believer,* and soon after, they formed Aerial Pictures. She was executive producer with Parkes on their television show *Birdland,* developed prior to their association with Amblin Entertainment.

MacDonald also executive produced *To Wong Foo, Thanks for Everything, Julie Newmar, How to Make an American Quilt, Twister,* and *The Trigger Effect.* She first joined Amblin Entertainment as executive vice president in 1994. She is currently co-head with Parkes of the Motion Picture Division of Dream Works SKG.

Walter F. Parkes

Producer Parkes is a three-time Academy Award nominee: as director/producer of the feature-length documentary *The California Reich* (1978); as writer, with Lawrence Lasker, of the original screenplay for *War Games* (1983); and as producer of *Awakenings* (1990), nominated for Best Picture.

Parkes' other credits include *Sneakers* (producer, co-writer), *Volunteers* (producer), *Project X* (producer, co-writer), and *True Believer* (producer). He executive produced *To Wong Foo, Thanks for Everything, Julie Newmar, How to Make an American Quilt, Twister,* and *The Trigger Effect.* Parkes joined Amblin Entertainment as president in 1994. He and Laurie MacDonald currently head the Motion Picture Division of DreamWorks SKG.

ACKNOWLEDGMENTS

Permission to reprint copyrighted material from the following sources is gratefully acknowledged:

Marvel Entertainment Group, Inc., for the use of original cover art from *The Men in Black* comic book, page 16, and the interview with Lowell Cunningham, page 18.

The Complete Guide to Mysterious Beings, by John A. Keel, the excerpt reprinted on page 22.

Ron Borst/Hollywood Movie Posters, for the poster of *Earth vs. the Flying Saucers,* page 17, and the photograph from *The Man From UNCLE,* page 19.

We thank the following for their special contributions:

At Amblin Entertainment/DreamWorks SKG: Glenn Williamson, Marvin Levy, Jerry Schmitz, Randy Nellis, Barbara Ritchie, Peter Stougart, Wendy Ryding, and Joy Johnson, for providing vital information and materials and assisting in various stages of development.

At Sony Signatures: Madelyn Hammond, Ban Pryor, Anita Frazier, Pat Kelly, Sharon Sartorius, Nikki Lichterman, and especially Jack Westerkamp, for their support, cooperation, and understanding of our needs and deadline pressures.

At Columbia Pictures, for their support and assistance throughout the development of this book: Barry Josephson, Robert Levin, Ed Russell, Susan Levin, Barbara Lakin, Holly Haines, Deb Bruenelle, Lisa Winkle, Noah Campbell, Violet Gonzalez, Stephen Zhawred, Ivy Orta, and Hortencia Gonzalez.

In the *Men in Black* production office: associate producer Steve Molen, for coordinating our contacts with the creative team; script supervisor Joe Park, for checking the published screenplay; and Jane E. Russell and Lisa Stone for their helpful production notes.

At Industrial Light & Magic, for their invaluable assistance: public relations director Ellen Pasternack, visual effects producer Jacqui Lopez, and visual effects supervisor Eric Brevig; and at Cinovation, make-up artist Rick Baker and his colleague Heidi Holicker.

As always, the dedicated and expert staffs of Walking Stick Press and Newmarket Press: Miriam Lewis and Joanna Lynch for design contributions; Keith Hollaman, Joe Gannon, and Reka Daniels, for editorial and production coordination; and especially Dawn Margolis, for developing the *Men in Black Agent's Manual* and providing creative support in many areas.

Much of the historical background on the Men in Black legends was adapted from material found in the website *The Paranormal Project* (at web address http://www.tenthmuse.com/paranormal/mib.html), to whose anonymous authors we are grateful.

Our deepest thanks to producers Walter F. Parkes and Laurie MacDonald, for their generous support and creative contributions; to screenwriter Ed Solomon, for his wonderfully readable script and his assistance in providing information about its development; to Lowell Cunningham, who created *The Men in Black* comic book and shared the story of how it happened; and to director Barry Sonnenfeld, for so thoroughly understanding the adventurous, comic, anything-is-possible spirit of *Men in Black*.

Esther Margolis, publisher, Newmarket Press

Diana Landau and Linda Herman,
Walking Stick Press

MIB

MEN IN BLACK